UNDERSTANDING
BRANDS

UNDERSTANDING
BRANDS

BY 10 PEOPLE WHO DO

EDITED BY DON COWLEY

KOGAN
PAGE

DISCLAIMER

The masculine pronoun has been used throughout this book. This stems from a desire to avoid ugly and cumbersome language, and no discrimination, prejudice or bias is intended.

First published in 1991
Reprinted in 1992

Kogan Page Limited
120 Pentonville Road
London N1 9JN

British Library Cataloguing in Publication Data
A CIP record for this book is available from the British Library.

ISBN 0 7494 0374 8

Typeset by Saxon Printing Ltd, Derby

Printed in England by Clays Ltd, St Ives plc

Contents

Acknowledgements

For help at some pretty crucial times:

Valerie Loizou

Victoria Pratt

Introduction

D O N   C O W L E Y

Don Cowley was one of the first of the new breed of strategic thinkers called Account Planners who emerged in advertising during the 1970s and revolutionised the way that brands and brand communication are developed in the UK. He has been planning director at FCB and Slaymaker Cowley White, and he has also been a managing partner at WCRS. He is currently planning director of Davies Little Cowley.

A regular speaker and writer on advertising and brand topics, he conceived and edited the Account Planning Group's first book How to Plan Advertising, *published in 1987.*

Introduction

DON COWLEY

The concept of a brand is probably the most powerful idea in the commercial world. Indeed, the way in which it provides a means of explaining the phenomena of business life, is in some ways analogous to the impact of Newton's theories on the physical sciences, when suddenly thinking people had a breathtakingly powerful means of understanding the world around them. However, the time-scale is different. Newton's work was absorbed some centuries ago, while our understanding of brands and their application to solving business problems is still very much in development.

The formal history of brands is in many ways a prosaic one, starting not all that many years ago when mass production and wider distribution led manufacturers to identify (or brand) their merchandise in a recognisable way, so as to offer a promise of consistent quality. But the real history of brands is much longer and more interesting. Brands truly understood are the things which patrol the boundary between people and the world outside them. Well before the industrial revolution people were acquiring swords, horses, estates, even countries, not only for their usefulness but because of what they projected about the person him or herself. In a deeper sense, people have always used objects not just to change outward impressions, but also to change things inwardly, ie to change themselves. Children's obsessions with trivial objects like, say, coloured pens, is instructive. Once they have acquired the desired, but frequently useless object, their interest disappears because they find that no amount of coloured pens makes you into a different person.

The same is sadly true in later life. The anticipation of owning a fast sports car is never matched by the reality. In truth, one car turns out to be much like another, and you're still the same person.

The science and art of branding has become much more valuable since its practitioners have learnt to expand the notion beyond the makers' mark and pure performance-based claims, to embrace the whole relationship between a product or service and its customers. So we are seeing a stirring of interest in brand thinking from all sorts of businesses – lawyers for example, who've only just begun to realise that vague concepts like 'reputation' can be sharpened by using the concepts of branding. Similarly, machine tool manufacturers have discovered that production directors are as susceptible to design values as the rest of us, so what a machine looks like can be as important as what it does.

We have also seen a stirring of recognition in another bastion of confined thinking – the political party. Both of the main British parties have fairly recently put an exploratory toe in the water, each with a redesign of their logo. For their own peace of mind they might do well to stop there. A really incisive analysis of the two parties as brands might well provide a vision which would be more than the party faithful could cope with. Extending that thought to cover some other time-honoured British institutions might also be painful. The Royal family would not necessarily find a totally dismal picture, but the Church of England would probably be wise to avoid the degree of self-knowledge that would be implied.

That said, the main territory which the authors of this book have addressed themselves to is the more normal area of marketing mass consumer brands. In contrast to the wider application of brand thinking to new kinds of problems, the quality of thinking in traditional packaged goods marketing has rather stagnated. Even in companies whose whole business is in packaged goods and whose advertising expenditures may exceed their whole pre-tax profit, it is not uncommon to hear marketing issues debated in such terms as 'What's our USP?', or 'Where's our positioning?' Such all-embracing phrases as brand image occur with regrettable regularity, as do such banalities as 'taking the high ground'.

The fault of such expressions as image, positioning, and even USP (unique selling proposition), is that they are fat words or phrases covering a multitude of possible meanings and brand phenomena. They can be made to mean whatever the speaker wants them to, so that lengthy debates can and do take place without sufficient precision of expression for effective communication to take place.

Interestingly, most of the concepts in regular use today were developed in much earlier decades. The USP dates back to Rosser Reeves in the 1940s. Brand image is very much associated with David

Ogilvy and the 1950s. Only slightly more recently, in the 1960s, J Walter Thompson London made a substantial step forward in brand analysis with their T-plan, which separates the common characteristics of a brand into three groups: knowledge, beliefs and emotional projections; but there has been little progress (at least publicly) since that time. The spread of account planning, firstly in London advertising agencies, but now on a much more international basis, has provided an enormous amount of good brand thinking. Unfortunately, most of that thinking has been bespoken to particular brands or types of brand. There have of course been brand consultants with patent methods, but by and large these have been too complicated and sometimes obscure to be adopted by the consumer marketing community as a whole.

It is surprising that no one has yet attempted to codify a modern approach to branding. To me, this seems more the result of a collective failure of nerve, than an impossible task, but perhaps in this new, less frenetic decade the industry will make some effective moves.

Which brings us to this book. Not that the authors have set out to do anything like suggest a new method of brand analysis, but I think there are a number of directional clues. For example, the first and third chapters, dealing as they do with some of the fundamental ideas in branding, both illustrate the many facets of a brand but in rather different ways. Sandwiched between them in chapter two, the author suggests a simple but, I suspect, rather powerful classification of brand values into product image, user image, occasion image and brand personality. Add to that the notion of saliency expressed as emotional closeness (rather than the normal unenlightening awareness measure), then I think you would probably have a pretty good starting point for examining the strengths and weaknesses of your brand.

Having analysed your brand's problem you are then stuck with the issue of what to do about it. The quantity of investment is potentially huge and the opportunities for making a mistake are ever present. Sound advice on media decision-making is offered by an industry leader in chapter 4. You should read it.

The subject of competition is an important one, which chapter 5 touches upon. Nearly all the markets that our authors refer to are highly competitive ones where the brand owner faces the constant prospect of losing share or losing margin, or unhappily finds that it's quite easy to make no money at all. The point about understanding your brand better is that it gives you a variety of different dimensions in which you can compete. A brand with a price advantage can simply be undercut, a brand with a performance advantage can be outflanked by technical development, but a brand with an emotional difference can potentially command a premium for ever. This may sound like a marketing truism, but how commonly is it forgotten?

If I were a brand manager (which I'm not), where I would look to make the biggest difference for the least amount of money is in packaging (chapter 6). Packaging is where brand marketing began, it is also where until very recently the least development in thinking took place. The view of the pack as a simple identifier was up to a few years ago the generally held perception of its role, but recent experience has demonstrated that packs are capable of a good deal more. The pack shape and surface is as much a medium for projecting brand values as the television commercial, and it has the bonus of being virtually free. The author talks about the idea of active packaging, by which she means packs which set out to make a communication as though the pack were itself an ad. The power of packaging to mould consumer perception is probably best demonstrated in own-label packaging where, with virtually no advertising for many categories, the private label brand's values are superior to the advertised alternatives. One possible outcome of the active packaging approach may be that it will provide an effective means for smaller brands to compete in markets where the advertising cost barriers to entry have conventionally been regarded as insuperable. Perhaps the career-minded account planner should take a closer look at the packaging industry. The toughest job in an advertising agency is undoubtedly that of the creative director. In chapter 7 the author illustrates the difficult task of reconciling creative inspiration with the brand owner's aspirations.

The 1980s' boom in takeovers and highly leveraged debt financing led to a sudden and completely new interest in the valuation of brands. Some of the takeovers, like the Nestlé acquisition of Rowntree, were the result of far-sighted thinking about the future dominance of multi-national branding; some were much more to do with shoring up perilously damaged balance sheets. That brands are financial assets, indeed in many cases representing the vast majority of the assets of many consumer marketing companies, has never been seriously doubted by marketing professionals. It only became an issue when people wanted to ascribe a specific value. If anyone doubts that this can be done, they should read chapter 8 of this book, and then send another copy to their financial director and auditors. From a brand marketing point of observation, accountancy bodies seem not to have covered themselves with glory in dealing with the brand valuation issue. The valuing of any kind of asset will always present difficulties, but that is no reason for ignoring it. Take Cadbury's for example. Do the products sell because of the name? Yes. Could another confectionery company make the same products? Of course. Could the brands be sold independently of the company? No reason why not, except humanitarian ones.

Brand valuation is not the only topic on which the accountancy profession has not distinguished itself. There have been a number of company failures where its conventional policing role has been found wanting. Although this issue is outside the scope of a book about brands, it is hard to avoid the conclusion that the accountancy profession needs to do some serious rethinking on more than one issue.

My reference to Nestlé is a reminder of the largest issue facing brand marketing, particularly UK advertising agencies, and more particularly the strategic specialists called account planners. British advertising has achieved acclaim over the last twenty years for the way it has broken the mould of mechanistic (implicitly American) advertising and communicated to its public with wit, charm, style and also, it has to be said, effect. Account planners helped develop this kind of advertising, particularly using the rich dialogue with the brands' (British) consumers that qualitative research can provide.

But the world is changing, the international brand is an inevitability. It will determine not just what we buy, but also our political structures; one of the reasons that Britain has joined the European Monetary System is because in a very large part, national economies can no longer be controlled domestically. The needs and ambitions of multi-national corporations are a force which both straddles national economies and rivals them for importance. The monetary ebbs and flows of their investment decisions are what determine governments' room for manoeuvre. Their objectives are becoming both long-term and completely global. Take the example of Toyota, with their new Lexus range. Currently in Europe this would be seen as inferior in brand values to Mercedes or BMW; but it must be regarded as highly likely that the continuing development of Lexus as a brand will mean that by the year 2000, Lexus will equal or even exceed those two German icon brands in consumer esteem.

It is also an inevitability that the way the brand is positioned and promoted will be increasingly the same in every country in the world. In chapter 9 the author draws on the rather spectacular simile of comparing the international brand with the Eiffel Tower. The point being that the brand will remain the same, even though the environment will vary.

My own feeling is that the international brand represents the biggest challenge in strategic brand and advertising planning. The qualities of the brand have to be sifted accurately enough to exclude the values which merely reflect local culture. Equally, having properly tied down the brand's own values, the task of effectively expressing them within the local culture of each country will remain. Many international brand owners will give up on the latter and simply run the same ad everywhere. Companies and ad agencies who truly understand their brands ought to be able to do better.

I have no doubt that we're moving into an era where the ability to understand and manipulate brands will become the key different-iator between consumer companies; but I do have some doubts about whether the brand skills required are sufficiently widespread to meet the industry's need.

In a small way, I hope this book can help.

CHAPTER ONE

Defining a Brand

PAUL FELDWICK

Paul Feldwick joined Boase Massimi Pollitt in 1974 after leaving Trinity College Oxford with a first in English. He is now head of account planning at the same agency, which has become BMP DDB Needham.

In 1988 and 1990 he was convenor of the judges for the IPA Advertising Effectiveness Awards, and edited Advertising Works *5 and 6. He has been chairman of the Association of Qualitative Practitioners, and is currently chairman of the Account Planning Group. He is a fellow of the Institute of Practitioners in Advertising.*

CHAPTER ONE

Defining a Brand

PAUL FELDWICK

Towards the end of 1989 the Marketing Society held a major conference in London. Its title was 'The Immortal Brand', and its publicity made prominent use of a quote from the Group Chief Executive of United Biscuits:

'Buildings age and become dilapidated.
Machines wear out.
People die.
But what live on are the brands.'

The visual design accompanying this theme was striking. The immortal brand was represented by a stylised, golden sun with a face on, perhaps reminiscent of an entertainment at the Court of *le roi soleil*. This rose above a classical montage of Greek temples, broken columns and Herculean statues. The metaphor is clear: the brand as deity, a sentient being whose existence transcends our merely human lifespan.

And indeed this is how we in marketing and advertising talk of brands. They have life cycles; they have personalities. In our research we personify brands, and find consumers can play the game. Unconsciously we credit the brand with some kind of absolute, platonic existence. Our mission is to *discover* (rather than invent) its 'core values' and abide by them. In fact, the brand is a rather primitive kind of god. If we keep its laws and pay regularly the tributes due (mainly advertising), fortune will smile on us – otherwise, disaster.

Now most of this is a way of saying valuable and important things about branding. Brands can 'live' longer than people. The metaphor of personality has been helpful, and I will later on make extensive use of it myself. But it may be worthwhile at the start of this book to

SOURCES OF ADDED VALUE IN BRANDING

Authenticity

Replicability

↓

Reassurance

↓

Inner
directed   Transformation of   Outer
                     experience   directed

↓

Differentiation

↓

ADDED VALUE

remind ourselves that it *is* only a metaphor. A brand may have
'personality', but it is not a person, still less a god on a cloud. You
cannot talk to it and it cannot answer you back. In fact, a brand has
no absolute or objective existence – nor are its 'core values' written
on a tablet of stone in the Gobi Desert. A brand is simply a collection
of perceptions in the mind of the consumer.

What I want to do in this chapter is to start from the consumer.
Why does this phenomenon called branding – about which we get so
mystical – exist at all? Presumably it satisfies certain needs on the
part of the consumer: but what are they? How does branding work,
and under what conditions?

The tentative answers in this chapter – and I regard it only as an
essay which I hope others may improve on – are rather complex.
Branding can be seen as satisfying various different needs, and
working at different levels and in different ways. What I will suggest
in fact has happened is that brands originally begin as a badge or
promise of certainty in an uncertain world, and that this offers simple
and functional benefits to any consumer. But because a brand offers
this kind of certainty, it also becomes a kind of currency for
consumers to carry out less obviously related kinds of transactions
with themselves and with each other. In a sense, consumers have
'hijacked' brands for their own purposes. But all the ways in which
brands can be used derive from the basic promise of certainty, and I
will therefore argue that we are talking about one coherent, if
complex phenomenon. Brands as a badge, and brands as personality
are aspects of the same thing.

At its simplest, a brand is a recognisable and trustworthy badge of
origin, and also a promise of performance.

A BADGE OF ORIGIN

All histories of marketing or advertising refer to the Bass Red
Triangle, registered as the first trade mark in England in 1876 and, I
am glad to say, still going strong. It will serve as a good example of
branding at its simplest – as a guarantee of authenticity.

This is something we rather take for granted, but it is of fundamental importance in underpinning the mechanisms of branding. When
we buy a jar of Hellmann's Mayonnaise, we can be fairly sure it *is* a
jar of Hellmann's Mayonnaise. Rigorous legislation in this country
prevents forgery or 'passing off'. When this was less true than today,
many packaging designs were as elaborate as banknotes, to dis-
courage forgery and emphasise authenticity ('None genuine without

this signature'). Once this confidence is breached, the symbols and hence the satisfaction of a brand lose their potency. (How am I to recognise a *real* Lacoste sports shirt nowadays?)

Many of the higher-value satisfactions of brands depend crucially on this belief in authenticity. This point will be particularly stressed in the section that follows later, on 'transformation'. In the meantime, just consider this: A fake Rolex watch may fool everyone else, but *it won't fool you*.

THE PROMISE OF PERFORMANCE

The other reason that we believe in brands is that, overwhelmingly, they keep their promises. If every bottle of Heinz Tomato Ketchup tasted different from the last, the brand would have no meaning. If consumers are prepared to forgive the exceptional bad experience from a trusted brand, this is because they know it is exceptional. On a familiar product the brand name offers a replicable degree, and kind, of customer satisfaction.

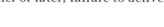 The product itself need not remain, literally, unchanged. Certain products, such as newspapers, change constantly by their very nature. Most successful brands continually improve or update their products to remain competitive, or to meet changed market requirements. But if the product does not reliably live up to the promise, the brand, however strong its history, eventually loses its force. Coca-Cola, one of the world's best-loved brands, provoked howls of betrayal with its ill-judged reformulation of 'New Coke'. Even in a market where we tend to think of 'image' transcending product reality, the poor quality of Jaguar cars which were built in the early 1970s did great damage to the marque's reputation, which was repaired with difficulty. Even a gradual decline in product performance can have the same effect, as when Cadbury's reduced the thickness of their Dairy Milk chocolate bar by imperceptible stages, until it was competitively vulnerable to the launch of Rowntree's Yorkie.

At best, a strong brand may provide a time-lag between the product becoming uncompetitive, and consumer rejection of it. In the early 1970s Cadbury's Smash users remained loyal to the brand, despite the launch of a technically superior product from Wondermash. This provided a breathing space for Cadbury's in which to match the new formulation: but it is unlikely that it would have gone on for ever. Sooner or later, failure to deliver renders a brand meaningless.

The extent to which product delivery ultimately underlies the strength of brands is often, I suspect, forgotten by those who subscribe to the myth of 'the brand in the sky'. But sooner or later, product realities will rewrite reputations, however powerful they are. How many years will it be before the aspirational luxury car becomes a Toyota or a Honda, rather than a Mercedes or a BMW? I suspect not many: and if you doubt it, look at the motorcycle market (or cameras, or hi-fi...).

At this stage the benefits to the consumer are clear. The brand offers a strong promise of both *authenticity* and *replicability*. Indeed without these, consumer decision-making would become a lottery and, probably, a nightmare.

But the promise is more than an aid to decision-making. A promise actually creates value in its own right, by enhancing the experience of owning or using the product.

The Value of Reassurance

Consider the satisfactions of owning a motor car. Many of these are tangible experiences: the comfort of the seats; the pleasure of driving it; its added comforts, such as air conditioning or a stereo; its beauty to the eye; its speed and performance, for those who like that sort of thing ....

But there are other requirements from a car which are less tangible. It is important, for example, that the car won't break down. The fact that it hasn't done so in the past is real; the expectation that it won't do so in the future is hypothetical. The degree of reassurance I personally feel as to whether the car will break down, when starting my journey, makes a major difference to my satisfaction as a user of the car. Branding can make a major difference to that reassurance. What the brand name does is translate a very hypothetical, negative kind of product superiority, into a real and immediate experience. I set out confident, relaxed, able to enjoy the trip. The value that I place on this feeling is part of the value that I may be prepared to pay for the brand, over and above the value I perceive in the nuts and bolts of the visible car. (For years, Volkswagen advertising in the UK has been founded on the brand's *reliability*: as a result the marque commands a significant price premium over comparable cars in its class.)

This is one example, but it is generally applicable to many other and less obvious situations. The reassurance I derive from the brand name (of performance, of authenticity) actually enhances the value I derive from the use of the product, over and above the physical evidence of my senses. While buying, cooking or serving my preferred brand of baked beans, I derive a heightened pleasure of anticipation long before I taste them. If serving drinks to guests, I am confident that a certain brand will be enjoyed by them, which puts me at my ease. If wearing clothes bearing the label of a famous designer, I feel more confident that they will look good under all circumstances – even if I lack confidence in my own judgement of style. In every case the added value consists in the fact that I can relax and enjoy the experience, confident that the brand *promises* that all problems are taken care of.

Transformation of Experience

What we have discovered here is that the subjective experience of using a *brand* can be different from the subjective experience of using an identical product without the brand reassurance. At one level, you could say this is just a matter of paying for peace of mind – not that we should underestimate this. But there's more to it. There is evidence that beliefs about the brand can actually affect perceptions of the physical product characteristics.

The simplest example is of the blind vs. branded product test. It can very commonly be shown that consumers tasting two food or drink brands comparatively may express a clear preference for one over the other (often the one with the greater market share), while the same product test conducted 'blind' shows no clear preference. Branding, in short, *transforms* the actual experience of using the product – and thereby adds to its value.

One of the most striking demonstrations of the real value to the consumer of the brand experience is found in the analgesics market, as reported by Cooper and Branthwaite in an article in *The British Medical Journal*.[1] Patients taking their own preferred brand of analgesic (as opposed to a chemically-identical own-label product) claimed faster relief from pain. Doctors recognise this as the *placebo* effect, and it demonstrates that certain symptoms respond to the *ritual* of taking medicine as much as to the physical substance. The blind vs. branded product test demonstrates that this principle is applicable in many other circumstances.

The idea of transformation is a very powerful one and reflects the way in which much advertising and branding works. In 1987 many people's imaginations were gripped by the story of the Nanking Cargo, a load of porcelain sunk for 200 years in the South China Sea. The items themselves are no different from much other porcelain already available: but the experience of owning or handling one of these bowls is rendered quite different by the knowledge of its extraordinary and romantic history. As a result such dishes sell for a considerable premium: the added value for which collectors will pay. The parallel with a commercial 'brand' is clear: both hinge on the *authenticity* of the goods.

It is commonly asserted that paying more 'for the name' is a foolish delusion on the part of the customer, and little more than a confidence trick on the part of the seller. Yet the benefit to the customer is a real enhancement of his experience of consumption, whether it consists in peace of mind or an imaginative experience.

To understand this we need to understand that the benefits sought by most consumers are subjective, and go a stage or two beyond the product's literal function. Charles Revlon used to say that others sold cosmetics, he sold *hope*. Parallel benefits can be imagined for any other type of product. People who buy toothpaste actually want *confidence* and *security* – that their teeth won't fall out, that their breath won't smell. People who buy tennis rackets or golf balls are buying the belief that they can win. A mother buying detergent is buying a way of presenting and showing affection for her family. Children selecting breakfast cereals are choosing *fun*... and so on. What is really on sale is an abstraction – and in all these cases, it will come from the brand, rather than the product. (Frequently, as the blind vs. branded tests show, the benefits are *projected* back on to the product itself.)

Differentiation and 'Brand Personality'

So the transformation that takes place is not merely an intensification of the experience, but an import of ideas which translate the simple function of the product into a relevant emotional metaphor. It is in this way that brand differentiation, and the idea of a brand 'personality' are created. If Persil is about 'caring', it evokes at one time both the perceived effect of the powder on the clothes (gentle and effective) and also the kind of emotions a mother may have about her family while washing their clothes (contrary to what cynics may think, such emotions are not entirely an adman's myth). In this way the experience of washing with Persil is qualitatively different from using, say, Ariel, and satisfies a different (perhaps a complementary) set of emotional needs from the process. Washing clothes is not after all an act which has to take place in the way in which we do it; it is part of a social context of relationships both within the family, and between the family and the world outside, and this creates needs beyond the merely functional.

In further work done by Cooper into the analgesics market, the enhanced effectiveness of certain brands on individuals can be related to the specific characteristics of *how* the brand was perceived to work. These were expressed through a role-playing exercise in which, for example, one brand behaved as soothing the pain away gently, the other as a powerful force attacking it.

It is when we enter this realm of differentiation that the metaphor of brand personality becomes extremely valuable. But it all develops naturally from the idea of consistency and familiarity. In dealing with people, 'personality' describes the ways in which we anticipate an individual will behave in particular circumstances. Of course, no one is totally predictable: but on the whole, they are predictable enough for human relationships to depend largely on this construct. Thus we create our friends, our acquaintances, and our enemies. The same is true of brands.

Consumers, as Stephen King[2] pointed out, can easily be encouraged to talk about brands in terms of human analogy – a technique still widely used, both qualitatively and quantitatively. What this really means is that consumers feel different relationships to different brands, depending on the type of subjective needs which the brands do or don't satisfy. Sometimes different brands appeal to different personality types; sometimes they fulfil complementary needs for the same person. In this way functionally similar products can remain competitive on grounds other than simple price.

To sum up our argument so far: a brand is fundamentally a promise, rendered credible by law and by experience. At one level this simply makes the decision process easier; at a higher level it can actually add to consumers' beneficial experience of a product, thus creating a value for which people may be prepared to pay.

The way in which the experience is transformed can be very particular to the brand, thus creating differentiation between similar products and the metaphor of personality.

Social Dimension

So far, we have (deliberately) talked as if the individual consumer and the brand manufacturer were the only two parties involved in this process. This has made the story simpler, but it is of course never true. Everything we have described so far has an added *social* dimension. An attitude towards a certain behaviour (following Fishbein)[3] is not simply determined by my own beliefs or experiences, but also by what I imagine other (relevant) people might think of the same thing. Our discussion of the satisfactions of owning a motor car was noticeably incomplete, because this element was left out. It may be helpful to take up this example again, in order to explore the various ways in which our decisions and perceptions can be affected by what we think other people think.

First there is a need for reassurance. Few people, in most situations, are prepared to trust their own judgement totally in isolation, without some reference to what others in the same situation believe (those few probably have a tendency to become either millionaires or bankrupts). In a complex and high investment decision such as choosing a car, buyers characteristically make this need overt by soliciting advice in the office or pub, and by buying car magazines. At the end of the day they will often find their choice assisted by the thought that the huge numbers of people like themselves buying Fords or Vauxhalls can't be wrong. In many markets this feeling of safety in numbers contributes to the reputation of the brand leader, and is not uncommonly exploited in advertising ('a million house-wives every day'...etc).

But this is not in itself the most important way in which others become involved in my purchase decisions. Patterns of consumption are not just driven by functional benefits – they are social statements which continually define or redefine our relationship with others, our position in society. This is true in all kinds of human society, by no means only those in which brands exist. Anthropologists (such as Mary Douglas[4]) have shown how in certain tribal cultures the ownership, production, giving and consumption of certain types of food define social relationships. I have basic functional needs (to eat, to keep warm), but what and how I eat, and what I wear are partly conditioned by what society deems appropriate (to my power, status, life-stage) and partly by what kind of role I wish to assume for myself. In the case of a car purchase, this creates strong pressures which may conflict with each other, and indeed with some of the functional criteria for a choice. All this would still hold true independent of brands: but brands are one of the key ways of defining and codifying the world, and so become an important part of the language in which these social statements are expressed. Because brands are authenticated, they become particularly robust currency for social exchange. Patterns of relative affluence, of peer group endorsement, of conformity or non-conformity, create strong social meaning for BMW vs. Mercedes, Volkswagen vs. Peugeot.

The social power of brands can be at its most overt in communal rituals of consumption such as beer drinking. Heavy drinkers of lager tend to be young working-class males, for whom the evening's 'session' is a highly-structured event with strong pressure to conform. In the context a brand of lager needs to be accepted by the group before it is OK to order it – Hofmeister, as an unknown brand, was unacceptable until George the Bear (an aspirational, surrogate group leader sharing in the group's sense of humour) positioned it.

It might also be important for the young lager drinker to be wearing the right clothes. Clothes are one of the most obvious social signs of conformity or non-conformity with a particular group, a phenomenon which of course exists separately from brands. In some contexts it might be a sufficient symbol to wear jeans; in others it might be necessary to wear a certain brand of jeans, particularly now that jeans are acceptable among a wide range of social groups and situations. Branding adds an extra level of clarity and complexity to the social language of clothes. Obvious parallels exist in many other markets: cigarettes, watches, shoes, and also household durables. (Why does your fridge have its name on the front?)

It is important to stress that the outer-directed value of a brand (as a badge to others) and the inner-directed value of the brand (as transformation of the user's experience) are not distinct from each other. They continually overlap, interact, and in some cases may even be different ways of looking at the same thing. Most designer labels, after all, are inside the clothes, not outside. A tie says 'Pierre Balmain', or 'Yves St Laurent' on the back, not the front. Realistically, most people will never see it or know what endorsement it carries. But because you feel you know what they would think of it *if they did*, you have the same (inner-directed) confidence or sense of style that comes from the name. The satisfaction of owning a particular make of car and knowing that it is socially regarded as a symbol of a certain kind of success can exist without reference to any other people actually being involved – 'it will remind you that your life has not been totally without success', as a famous ad for Jaguar once put it. Is this inner-directed or outer-directed? And does it matter? The social dimension is so pervasive in branding that it is hard to separate it out, and probably a fruitless exercise to do so.

If I had to venture a one-line definition of branding, perhaps to sum up what may have seemed like an over-complex analysis, it would be to do with 'the intangible values created by a badge of reassurance'. The intangible values may be simple (peace of mind, structuring choice) or increasingly complex (gaining the approval or approbation of others, or actually defining the experience of the product itself). In the majority of cases – possibly in all cases – the satisfactions of branding are potentially a combination of these, in varying proportions. Some recent authors[5] have suggested that brands can be classified into those which are simple, non-emotional badges of product quality, and those which offer rich emotional or symbolic values. This must have some validity in so far as some brand choices involve an important rational component related to product characteristics (eg garden tools), while others are more obviously concerned with differentiating essentially similar products (say, cigarettes). But it seems to me simplistic in that it ignores the intangible, often indeed emotional benefits which branding confers on superficially 'functional' product choices – and also the fact that emotional or socially symbolic brand values are generally based on some genuine (if perhaps historic) product qualities.

An example may illustrate the first of these points. You might consider paint to be a very functional product, where the brand name simply stands for a particular chemical composition, and qualities of covering power, durability etc. Yet when people paint they do far more, usually, than simply cover their walls. First, they derive a powerful sense of transformation and renewal from the decorating process – brand values of a less tangible sort, 'freshness', 'naturalness' become potentially important. Second, if they apply the paint themselves (the most usual procedure) there is a strong sense of pride and achievement in 'doing the job properly' – and part of this is the choice of the 'right' brand of paint. To be seen as 'the one experts use' can be a powerful discriminator. This is, of course, underpinned by consistent product quality: but nuances of covering power or durability (which is a promise for the future anyway) are in themselves of secondary importance. By consistently making use of ideas like these in advertising, Dulux has for many years dominated the UK paint market. It may remind us that even in apparently very functional markets (washing-up liquid, kitchen towels, bathroom cleaners, etc) product performance is still a very subjective matter.

Even in industrial purchasing decisions, which we might imagine to be completely 'rational', difficult or complex choices are likely to be referred to beliefs about the suppliers' reputation – or quite likely influenced by the perceptions of other relevant managers. 'No one ever got fired for buying IBM' ran a famous slogan. The mechanics of branding are essentially the same here as anywhere.

Branding begins by satisfying a basic human need for control and reassurance. Because it offers consistency in an otherwise uncertain world, the brand then has the potential to become a tool for dividing up the world, and a medium of social exchange. In offering

[29]

reassurance and in creating rituals of consumption, branding always creates value to the consumer *beyond* the merely functional.

REFERENCES

1. Branthwaite, A and Cooper, P (1981) 'Analgesic effects of branding in treatment of headaches', *British Medical Journal*, 282.

2. King, S (1970), 'What is a brand?', JWT.

3. For a description of Fishbein's expectancy value model, see Tuck, M (1976) *How Do We Choose?*, Methuen, ch 6.

4. Douglas, M (1982) *In The Active Voice*, Routledge and Kegan Paul.

5. De Chernatony, L and McWilliam, G (1989) 'Representational brands and functional brands: the strategic implications of the difference', Admap, March.

Accessing the Brand through Research

WENDY GORDON

After a five-year apprenticeship in South Africa working for J Walter Thompson, Market Research Africa and Pepsi Cola, Wendy emigrated to the UK where she specialised in qualitative market research. Between 1978 and 1981, a period which coincided with the development of the account planning function in advertising agencies, she set up a unit within the Schlackman Research Group specialising in advertising development research. So successful was this that in 1981 she formed The Research Business with her partner Colleen Ryan. The Research Business Group is now the largest independent market research company in the UK, ranking eighth in the AMSO league table.

Wendy is a frequent presenter of papers at advertising and research conferences, as well as teaching on industry courses. She is co-author of the user-friendly book Qualitative Market Research – A Practitioner's and Buyer's Guide, *which was published in 1988.*

CHAPTER TWO

Accessing the Brand through Research

WENDY GORDON

A whole new language has grown up around brands – brand husbandry, brand abuse, brand neglect, brand stretching, brand engineering, and umbrella branding – these are only a few. An observer from another discipline might well draw the conclusion that brand owners have become alerted to the true value and potential of their brands and are therefore making the most of the competitive brand opportunities that are presented. Not so. Despite the new language of brand development, too many brand owners and their marketing or advertising advisors still think in very basic terms, like USP, or first-class brand image.

Mental effort, marketing energy and financial resources continue to be invested in brand differentiation through tangible product or service attributes; only lip-service is paid to the importance of the emotional values underpinning a brand. This results in a mental brand framework in which brand owners compete along the same dimensions as their competitors, rather than taking the opportunity to compete on a different level.

Some brand owners have recognised that the battle can be fought on a different plane. For example, without the use of advertising in the conventional sense, The Body Shop has achieved an extremely competitive brand positioning through the powerful cohesiveness of its vision of environmental integrity. Its competitive appeal for consumers lies not principally in the attributes of its products (eg good value, natural/herbal products), which have been copied by many other brands and retailers, but in taking the emotional high ground of care and concern for the environment. Oxo is another famous example of brand owners understanding that the competitive edge for the brand lay in holding an identity mirror to the consumer,

[33]

who sees herself and her family realistically reflected in Katie's family, and thus the brand.

Although these brand owners have demonstrated ably the power of competing at a different level from their competitors, many have not. Why? Primitive research methodology is one of the prime culprits:

> 'Traditional consumer market research approaches are too shallow. They do not allow you to understand what the brand means to consumers at a deep level – they do not let people express themselves creatively – we do not find group discussions and U&A studies useful anymore.'
> *(Hugh Davidson, The Marketing Society Conference 1989)*

The frustration underlying this comment is due to many factors, such as the structure and status of the research function within companies, the allocation and size of budgets, and the demand for instant results. On another level, the underlying reason is simple.

Researchers continue to design quantitative research with no understanding of how consumers relate to brands. Time after time questions are asked which have little or no chance of accessing the emotions underlying a brand. This is because questions are used which reflect the agenda that governs the lives of brand owners – brand and advertising awareness and recall, competitive market shares, movements in brand image in response to marketing or advertising spend, and purchase propensity are all examples. Research assumes that these items on the marketing agenda can be simply translated into direct questions to the consumer. This is a fallacy.

Conventional qualitative research is often no different. Marketing agendas are translated into group discussion guides, studies are commissioned to provide answers to tactical questions relating to packaging, advertising, brand extensions, product changes, competitive activity, and answers are required within two – three weeks.

Usually these studies consist of four – six group discussions, each lasting a little over an hour. Despite the battle cry of qualitative researchers that they are the only researchers who are really able to uncover how consumers feel, think or react, it is simply impossible to understand the essence of a brand within the constraints of this type of study.

THE LIMITATIONS OF CONVENTIONAL RESEARCH

The starting point for the development of a competitive brand strategy is to employ research to understand how the brand is viewed by its consumers at a key point in time and to take an inventory of its assets and liabilities, opportunities and threats. This involves interrogating existing research data, before commissioning any new studies. One of the first steps is to acknowledge that conventional research thinking and measures have inherent limitations which not only impede an understanding of the brand's current positioning, but can be dangerously misleading. Like road signs, there are a number of research signs which should signal caution immediately and, therefore, the need to proceed with due care, attention and control.

The danger signs are:

Brand   *Brand image*   *Purchase*   *Fat words*
awareness   *intentions*

Brand Awareness – a Simplistic Measure

The relationships consumers have with brands differ in terms of closeness or distance, intensity and time-frame. Some brands have an everyday presence in our lives, for instance Nescafé or Persil, while others have a more peripheral presence, correlated perhaps with infrequency of purchase (Atora) or low emotional involvement (Applause). There are some brands we feel intense about (BMW, Cadbury's) while other brands leave us coolly indifferent. Brands, too, have a temporal positioning in our mental maps of product categories – Cinzano is positioned in the past because it is a brand associated with teenage drinking, whereas Lanson might be positioned in the future – a relationship that might happen, but has not yet. Being positioned in the past is not automatically a disadvantage. Many brands, such as Hovis, Old Spice and Ribena, are perceived in this way, yet hold enormous appeal for certain consumers. It is the interrelationship between intensity, time-frame, and closeness–distance, which indicates whether or not consumer response is positive or negative, active or passive.

The term *salience* defines the nature of the consumer–brand relationship described in this way. Salience is a far more valuable tool for understanding what a brand means, than brand awareness. The latter is a simple and often abused piece of brand information, which simply tells a manufacturer the readiness with which a brand springs to mind or is acknowledged when prompted with a brand list. The reason that this data is often abused is that it is taken to mean salience, that is, the importance the brand holds for the consumer. Brand awareness is useful for understanding what is happening to a new brand, but is of no value when used for well-established brands where almost 100 per cent of the sample are aware of the brand, eg banks, petrol/oil companies, mainstream teas.

Brand Image – a Complex Concept

It may seem strange to think of brands as existing *only* in consumers' heads. Although the manufacturer or service company is able to change the nature of the product itself, its distribution and presentation, the *added values* the brand has (functional and non-functional) are built in the minds of consumers. New entrants to established product categories require an enormous financial investment to build these values, which ensure that a target group of consumers are able to share a similar pattern of specific belief systems about a brand.

All of us have a melting pot of impressions in our minds about particular brands. The hotch-potch of visual images, sounds, feelings, smells and tastes that are connected with Perrier, for example, stem from direct experience, observation, past and present advertising, packaging, promotions *and* media coverage. The brand image of Perrier (or any brand) is very difficult to grasp hold of in its entirety, both by the individual in whose head it resides, as well as those of us who wish to extract it in order to examine it.

Over the past 20 years, qualitative research methodologies, techniques and approaches have moved on as researchers began to understand how consumers responded to purchase environments, brands, advertising, packaging, direct mail and PR. Quantitative research, however, particularly in the area of measurement of brand images, has remained firmly stuck with 1960s thinking, hoist by its own petard — the need for standardisation and replicability. Attitude statement batteries on tracking studies, particularly, demonstrate a complete lack of understanding of how to measure the values of a brand. The statement measures are often meaningless, bearing little or no relationship to the product area in question in terms of consumer motivations, behaviour and discriminating attitudes.

Dulux and Crown, two famous brands of paint, scored identically on a tracking questionnaire across most of the attitude statements, including 'wide range of colours'. This was perplexing, particularly as the long-running advertising campaigns were so different. Qualitative research revealed that the phrase *was* relevant to both brands, but in consumers' minds Dulux was visualised as a wide range of pastel colours, whereas Crown was associated with a wide range of brighter colours. There are endless examples of attitude statements on tracking studies remaining unchanged over long periods of time. Sometimes it is due to the fact that brand images are slow to change, often trailing far behind advertising or marketing activity, but mostly it is because current measurement techniques are too insensitive to pick up emotional rather than rational changes in image. It would therefore be wise to interrogate the attitude battery being used on your brand to ensure you understand what is the *exact* consumer interpretation of the statement you are tracking.

We therefore need to be absolutely clear what we are seeking to understand when we talk about brand image – what facets to explore and then measure, and how to provide consumers with the kind of help necessary to express the complexity of feelings about a brand.

Purchase Intentions – a Meaningless Average

Marketing and advertising in the western world is a process designed to influence consumer behaviour. Complex though it is, and little though we understand how it works, the combined efforts of marketing and advertising activity are expected to encourage consumers to buy/consume/choose one brand rather than its competitors. So obvious. But consumers are often unaware, consciously at least, as to why they do or don't use/buy/choose a particular brand. Asking for this kind of information in a direct way is like shouting loudly at a foreigner in the belief that he will then understand English more easily.

Examine your own buying behaviour. You may buy a brand out of sheer habit. You are on automatic pilot when you buy it and do not stop to evaluate whether or not a change in behaviour is needed. Another brand may be bought because of an internal feeling of compulsion – it would not be acceptable to serve an unknown, cut-price brand of whisky to business colleagues whom one wanted to impress. A brand may excite your curiosity because of word-of-mouth recommendation or advertising, such as Radion, resulting in a purchase 'just to see if what they say is true', or a brand may be bought out of indifference because of a belief that all the brands in the category offer the same benefits.

Understanding purchase behaviour involves more than the application of five-point rating scales such as:

I definitely will buy
I am fairly likely to buy
I might or might not
I am fairly unlikely to buy
I am definitely unlikely to buy

or applying this kind of question in a qualitative research environment. Such questions *do* yield answers and, when applied to large numbers of consumers, even provide means, averages and standard deviations. But what do they really mean? Can you, taking the examples given previously, numerically average the diverse emotional states which underpin buying behaviour, namely habit, compulsion, curiosity or indifference?

There is far more to be learned about brand values by paying attention to the internal emotional rules which govern behaviour – any behaviour – whether trying, buying, repeat buying, consuming, lapsing, or rejecting, than by accepting simplistic numerical or quasi-numerical measures of purchase intention.

Fat Words – the Danger of Complacency

Each of the authors contributing to this book is involved in the brand business. Each represents a different perspective. Each of us needs to communicate our expertise and knowledge about a brand to others in a way that causes successful change. The main stumbling block to effective communication between us all and between ourselves and consumers is the personal meaning of words. If a brand is described as 'stylish, sophisticated yet accessible' or 'warm and confident', how do we each interpret this cluster of words? We forget that many words are 'fat', that they carry a weight of different meanings depending on who you are. Confidence for a 16-year-old girl in Newcastle is a different feeling from the word used by a successful female executive, a young creative team in London, or a 40-year-old marketing director.

We need to question words which are so integral to the process of understanding brand values. It is only by asking for clarification and by using analogies and examples, that we can be sure that we understand whether consumer values match our own.

There *are* ways of reaching below the surface of words to the underlying emotion, by accessing the sensory basis of the word. All words have a structure which can be dissected through sensitive research questioning techniques. The word confidence, in relation to the brand Charlie, is primarily concerned with pacey movement (bubbly, active), a warm temperature (friendliness and accessibility), and colour (bright but natural). It is a confidence that emanates from youthfulness. The confidence of Chanel, in comparison, is slow in pace (measured, reserved), cool in temperature (elegant and aloof), and subdued. It proclaims confidence emanating from wealth. Without this kind of sensory clarification, a brand strategy has little chance of effective execution (advertising, packaging, promotions, PR) which matches the needs of its target consumers.

A FIVE-PART SYSTEM FOR INTERROGATING A BRAND

Before providing a simple system for the analysis and valuation of a brand image, it is necessary to pick our way through a confusing array of jargon, which is written into market research objectives, conclusions and recommendations, communication strategy documents and creative briefs.

These are terms such as 'brand image', 'user image', and 'brand personality', which are often used interchangeably because everyone assumes that his understanding of the phrase is exactly the same as that of the person with whom the discussion is taking place. Since these terms are crucial to the in-depth understanding of what a brand *means*, it is necessary to define them.

Brand image and user image are the two oldest terms, and have been in use since the 1960s. Brand personality is a newer concept, and has a particular contribution to make in today's world of brand parity, when sometimes the only difference between brands is image-rather than product-related.

What is a brand image? The J Walter Thompson directory of market research terminology, *From Acorn to Zapping*, defines brand image as:

'The total impression created in the consumer's mind by a brand and all its associations, functional and non-functional.'

Brand image is an umbrella term, encompassing a number of image dimensions, of which user image is one. Rather like a diamond with many facets through which the true worth of the stone is judged, a brand image is described and valued by examining different facets: user image, occasion image, product image, brand personality.

A user image can be defined as the kinds of people believed by the consumer to be the most likely buyers/eaters/drinkers/users of the brand. This term reflects the marketing relationship between a brand and its consumers. The manufacturer has defined the target market, and a member of this target market recognises that he *is* or *is not* the addressee of the brand communication. His views as to who is the likely consumer of the brand may or may not mirror the intentions of the manufacturer.

If there is congruity, then consumers tend to express the user image in terms such as 'people like me' (use/buy the brand), but if there is dissonance, then the user image offers no point of identification in terms of its demographic or attitudinal profile.

The term 'brand personality' is quite a different concept. It is a metaphor for the emotional relationship that exists between a consumer and a brand. A brand personality is a shorthand way of describing the nature and quality of the consumer response to a brand. Thus, understanding that Domestos is like 'A knight on a white horse coming to save me from evil'; or 'A good policeman chasing the baddies from the world' clearly explains the relationship between consumers and Domestos – it is a saviour. However, this information alone is insufficient, because not all segments of the target market respond positively to this type of authority. Vortex users, for instance, respond to this personality with hostility – experiencing the brand as old-fashioned and paternalistic; whilst current users of the brand respond with affection, warmth and gratitude.

A brand personality can be well or poorly formed. Obviously new brands have unformed personalities, but an 'old' brand can also have a poorly-formed personality because of lack of consistent communication over the years, or insufficient support. Brands can have stable or unstable personalities across demographic sectors or geographic boundaries. Coca-Cola, for example, has a stable brand personality across national and regional boundaries. Some brand personalities match consumer needs and desires, while others do not.

Having defined these two components of a brand image (user image and brand personality), the next task of this chapter is to introduce a simple model for understanding a brand. Like all models, it is an oversimplification. Just as a map is not the same thing as the territory it describes, it nonetheless helps to direct the traveller from point A to point B with ease.

So a brand image can be understood by examining five different facets:

1. user image
2. occasion image
3. product image
4. brand personality
5. salience.

User Image

The user image of a brand is usually understood by asking questions such as 'judging from this advertisement, who do you imagine is most likely to buy Brand X?', or 'Thinking of Brand X, what kinds of women do you think buy it?' These questions lead to demographic descriptors of the perceived consumer. For example, a user image might be described in terms of age (young, old, teenagers), socio-economic group (eg wealthy businesspeople, middle class, working class) region (eg North, South) or life-stage (eg mums with kids, new home-owners), all of which can sometimes be qualified by lifestyle characteristics (eg health conscious, 'yuppy', environmentally aware).

An alternative to asking straightforward questions, is to design a visual collage board which shows a range of women (or men, couples, children, families, types of homes), cut out of magazines or news-papers. Consumers are asked to select those images which they associate with the brand and then to give the reasons for choice of a particular image or images. The advantage of this kind of stimulus material is that it can be used in qualitative *or* quantitative research, and generates answers that extend well beyond demographic descriptors.

An example is shown on page 42 of a range of women who might (or might not) be purchasers of specific brands of fruit juice. Table X shows that brands A and B are associated with very different users. Table Y shows the reasons behind the choice of user. Brand B is significantly more frequently associated with women who are health-aware than Brand A, which has an older, more affluent user image.

Table X Images chosen			Table Y Reasons for choice of image		
	Brand			*Brand*	
	A	**B**		**A**	**B**
	78	78		78	78
	%	%		%	%
G	37	47	Health-conscious	46	64
J	19	32	Well-off	15	–
L	32	9	Older, middle-aged	12	5
B	17	9	Afford expensive		
H	21	12	brands	–	10
			Classy, posh	9	–
			Buy best quality	10	–
			Young/modern	4	16

A careful distinction must be made between identification and aspiration. Say, for example, a downmarket woman with children describes the user image as 'upmarket, health-conscious young couples without children'. Is this an indication of non-identification, or is it aspirational? In other words, although the consumer may not actually see herself in this way, she might very much like to do so. The user image in this case is motivating. This is an example of the importance of reaching below the meaning of words to the underlying emotion, which in the example described, may be desire rather than hostility. Both qualitative and quantitative approaches often fail to perform this essential task of differentiating between identification and aspiration.

The important fact to understand about user image is that it is a two-way relationship. The communication flows from manufacturer to consumers, who evaluate the brand and its clothing (advertising, packaging, distribution, promotion) and draw logical conclusions about the marketing and/or advertising strategy. Consumers in the early 1990s are able to understand intended strategies, and often do so with surprising accuracy and sophistication.

A description of the user image of a brand is not always sufficient. The fact that Brand X is thought by consumers to be bought by young, modern housewives is only part of the equation. We need to know how consumers in the target market *respond* to this image. Does it confirm their existing beliefs about the brand, or does it cause re-evaluation? If the latter, is the re-evaluation in a positive or negative direction?

Occasion Image

Like user image, an occasion image consists of the beliefs consumers hold about the times and/or occasions on which the brand is eaten/drunk/consumed. For example, brandy is believed by many consumers to be drunk in the evening when relaxing or unwinding, whereas vodka has a more pub/party occasion image. Questions designed to describe occasion image tend to produce rational answers, eg daytime, evening, at home, at parties and so on. As with user image, it is far more useful to design a collage board showing a range of different kinds of occasions, to explore the relationship of a brand to a situation or mood. For example, mainstream blended whiskies are associated with sociable occasions, but what does this mean – drinking with mates in a pub, with a mixed group of friends in someone's home, a wedding celebration, after a business meeting, with a special friend at home? Visual collage boards enable researchers and brand owners to understand the subtle moods which define a brand's identity (in a competitive context). Occasion images rely on a wide range of impressions resulting from direct experience with the brand, observations of other users, and all the advertising, packaging or promotional cues which indicate occasion appropriateness.

Product Image

Product image is the most frequently used image dimension, and is often equated with brand image, to the detriment of a deeper understanding of the nature of a brand. Consumers have beliefs about the physical or functional characteristics of a product or service which may or may not reflect its true functional attributes. For example, in a blind product test, Brand A may perform *as well as* Brand B in terms of authenticity of flavour, richness of taste, quality and colour and yet in a branded product test, Brand A outperforms Brand B on taste, flavour and quality attributes. Typical product characteristics include: good quality, good value for money, authenticity of flavour, freshness. For non fmcg brands, service characteristics are often more relevant (eg friendly, efficient, expert).

WHISKY BRANDS – SCOTLAND			
	Brand A	*Brand B*	*Ideal*
	%	%	%
Strength of flavour	4.74	3.91	4.79
Fiery/mild	3.37	3.63	3.23
Real Scotch taste	5.06	4.24	5.54
Quality	5.10	3.90	5.80

Product attributes explored in qualitative research or measured by quantitative research, differ by product catagory. The results in the table above show the mean ratings on a series of six-point rating scales for two brands of whisky, and illustrate that Brand A matches the characteristics of an ideal whisky significantly more closely than Brand B.

Often, differences between brands across functional product attributes simply reflect market share, rather than consumer acknowledgement of real product differences.

The reason perhaps that the product image has become synonymous with brand image and is so often paid attention to by manufacturers, retailers and financial services, is that these consumer beliefs are seemingly within the total control of the marketing process. If consumers believe Brand A to be 'too dark' for a coffee, then all that needs to be done is to lighten its colour, or if this is not possible, to inform the target consumer that darkness is a product advantage. The problem with this simplistic line of reasoning is that force of logical argument does not necessarily change consumer perceptions. When British Rail ran advertisements in the press showing that 99 per cent of trains on a certain day left and arrived on time, this rational information did not change the attitudes and beliefs of the target market, who persisted in believing in the inefficiency of British Rail on the emotional grounds that '*my* train yesterday was late'.

Brand Personality

Whether quantitative or qualitative, a brand personality is elicited through questions like, 'if Knorr were to walk into this room as a person, what kind of person do you imagine?'

The answers can vary:

'Rather old-fashioned, not very active, conservative, dull colours, not young. Someone who is older than their years. A family person who has little time, energy or money to spend on herself';

or:

'Warm and friendly, colourful. Dressed in unusual clothing ... likes to be noticed.'

The fact that Knorr has both a positive *and* a negative personality requires further interrogation, in order to provide actionable decisions:

- What is the Knorr brand personality across user groups? How consistent is it?
- Which are the key characteristics of the Knorr personality that differentiate it from its competitors? Colourfulness? Energy?
- How do consumers respond to the personality of Knorr – do they feel special? Creative? Safe? Bored?
- How can the creatives (pack designers) be given help in executing the desired personality?

Brand personality is often the facet through which subtle differences between brands can be observed. In many tracking studies, conventional image batteries which focus on product image dimensions fail to show differences between brands, whereas both qualitative research and tailor-made quantitative brand personality studies are able to show marked differences.

Brand personalities are elicited through the use of projective questioning techniques, which are most usually employed in qualitative research studies, but are increasingly used in the more innovative forms of quantitative research.

Projective techniques are not psychological tests which result in Freudian mumbo-jumbo, but an invaluable tool for reaching below superficial, rationalised responses in a way that is perfectly acceptable to respondents themselves. The main point about projective techniques is that *respondents* (not the researcher) describe and interpret their own individual responses. Projective techniques work by encouraging the respondent to 'make sense' of an unstructured stimulus which allows a great number of solutions. On the basis that we all 'put something of ourselves into everything we do', the completed task reveals something about its doer.

The projective techniques of most help in describing brand personalities are: words and pictures; brand personalities; psychodrawing; video collages. A few brief sentences are given on each.

Words and pictures: a large number of scrap pictures and words, cut from magazines or newspapers, are given to respondents in a group discussion. The task is to create a collage of those words or pictures that 'fit' the brand. The reasons behind the choice of images is explained to the group moderator by the respondents.

Brand personalities: this has already been touched upon. Respondents are encouraged to imagine a brand and its competitors as human beings, and to describe their appearance, behaviour patterns and effect on those who meet each one. It is both amusing for respondents and revealing to imagine the brand personalities at a party – which brand is the host? Who talks to whom? Who is the wallflower? This reveals a great deal about perceptions of the competitive environment.

Psychodrawings: respondents are encouraged to draw a brand in order to explore which graphic elements most strongly contribute to its identity, or to draw their feelings about a particular product.

This technique is particularly appropriate for children or teenagers who are often more easily able to express feelings visually, rather than finding words to articulate a complex series of emotions. Adults, too, respond very well to the task, provided the moderator is experienced.

Video collages: a sequence of moving images edited from a range of commercials or film material is made into a short film (less then one minute) with an optional voice-over, music or verbal component. The advantage of video over visual collages is that moving images are more effective in conveying tonal qualities such as pace, temperature, movement, as well as subtleties of a brand personality, eg aggressive, assertive, competitive, determined or enthusiastic.

The measurement of brand personality is one of the most exciting areas of development in quantitative image research. For the first time, brand personalities can be statistically soundly described, and demographic or brand user subgroups compared, without loss of understanding of the emotional values of the brand.

In a study on the key personality differences between the *Guardian*, *The Times* and the *Independent* conducted among 100 BC1, age 20–30, working males and females, the following personality profiles emerged for each brand:

The Times
● Likes to win
● Follows rules
● A leader
Moderate/slow-paced, cool

Guardian

- A good listener
- Thoughtful
- Peaceful

Moderate/slow-paced, temperate

Independent

- Friendly
- Happy
- Likes a challenge
- Honest
- Likes change

Moderate/fast-paced, warm

The data summarised above, showed that *The Times* is seen to be a leader, competitive but not rule breaking, while the *Guardian* offers a more receptive and passive personality – contrasted by the *Independent*, which has a personality profile which is sociable, flexible, ambitious and honest.

Each personality can be further qualified by showing how consumers experience the three brands. *The Times* comes across as a cooler and slower-paced brand than the *Independent*, which is warmer and more pacey. The table below summarises the adjectives which differentiate the three newspaper brands in terms of 'how the personality makes me feel'.

	Guardian	*The Times*	*Independent*
Base	100 %	100 %	100 %
Feelings			
Overshadowed	9	41	21
Proud	5	18	21
Intelligent	48	41	64
Irritated	39	34	9
Safe	27	36	25
Defensive	18	21	11
Bored	25	27	–

The response to the *Independent* is very positive – the brand rewards its target market, who feel proud and intelligent to be seen in its company. *The Times*, on the other hand, elicits a polarised response – although a proportion feel safe with the brand, others feel intimidated. The *Guardian* also elicits a polarised response.

Often it is a combination of the brand personality and the user image which provides the clearest differentiation between brands. Comparing the Vauxhall and Ford marques (irrespective of model) among a male sample of company car 'user choosers', the following patterns emerged from the quantitative data.

	VAUXHALL	**FORD**
User image	reliable solid family person	ordinary everyday young
Brand personality	reliable rule follower well behaved (*Cautious trait*)	friendly easily pleased entertaining (*Sociable trait*)
Consumer response	safe relaxed pleased or indifferent not intelligent moderate-slow (pace)	relaxed happy affectionate fast-moderate (pace)

Ford appears to be a sociable and pacey brand which elicits a warm consumer response. It has a youthful but very accessible user image. Vauxhall is a more conventional and slower-paced brand which elicits a polarised consumer response, probably because of its older and more established user image.

Salience

Salience forms a linchpin that cements the other image facets in place. It is only by understanding the importance of the brand for different groups of consumers that we can interpret with confidence whether the user, occasion and product images, as well as the brand personality profile, are motivating or not.

Salience, from the consumer point of view, is a complex emotion made up of past, present or future (fantasy) experiences of the brand, strength of feeling and inclination to use, buy or try it. Salience thus has time-related, intensity and motivational components. You either feel distant from or close to a brand, you feel so strongly or weakly and it has a temporal meaning for you. If you examine your feelings about Ribena, Just Juice, Kia Ora or Del Monte you will notice that your awareness differs in type – from present relevance, to future interest to past indifference or even past nostalgia. You also feel degrees of closeness or distance towards these brands.

One of the most interesting developments in the study of communication in recent years has been the discovery that memories are recorded and stored with reference to time; otherwise how would we know the difference between past, present and future? In his book *The Man Who Mistook His Wife For A Hat* (Picador, 1986), Oliver Sachs described the case of Jimmy G who had an impairment or dysfunction such that whatever was said or shown to him, and whoever he met, was forgotten in a few seconds' time. Jimmy lived a life of isolated impressions – a life without purpose.

The fascinating aspect of this work is that time is literal, not merely metaphorical. Time is a way of storing information in the brain, and most of us store time in a linear way. You may have noticed that as people talk, you can understand what they are doing mentally by carefully listening to their temporal language patterns. When you say 'turn your back on the problem', 'put that aside', 'he turned towards her', these are simply verbal manifestations of how you physically place (and therefore classify) people, events or things. Most of us are able to represent time spatially, and for many the past is behind, the present near and in the front, and the future, some distance away, to the right. (Caution – this is a generalisation and probably only applies to people whose native language contains temporal tenses.)

In the course of recent quantitative brand studies, we have come to believe that brand saliency can be defined as the emotional distance between a consumer and a brand over a time continuum. By introducing consumers to a simple time–line diagram, and allowing them time to do the task, they are easily able to place, spatially, up to seven or eight brands. The competitive brand positionings are then coded using a template.

This type of information adds depth to standard awareness data, and is extremely useful in discriminating between brands by establishing emotional closeness or distance, as well as locating the brands in a past, present or future time-frame.

[49]

To summarise, the strength of this five-part model of brand analysis is that it demonstrates how a brand image is constructed and how the different facets interrelate, thus revealing which aspects of the brand image offer the most competitive edge.

NEW BRAND THINKING

In recent years there has been a great deal of new work into the theory of communication – in both personal and business contexts. Many of the business books you find at airports, or the endless management courses and seminars that land on your desk, are manifestations of the growing awareness of the relationship between effective communication skills and successful management.

To date, little of this new knowledge seems to have been applied to the communication process of brands.

There are two concepts of communication which have particular application for brand development:

- the hierarchy of communication levels
- reframing a negative image.

The Hierarchy of Communication Levels

Mass communication such as advertising, in particular, can be understood in the same way as individual human communication – the process and levels of communication are similar. Humans communicate at a number of different levels (called neurological levels in NLP (Neuro-linguistic programming)).

Vision (I promise), eg 'I have a dream' (Martin Luther King).
Identity (I am), eg I am a caring, gentle person.
Belief (I believe), eg I believe in state education.
Capability (I can), eg I play tennis and cook Japanese food.
Behaviour (I do), eg I work full-time.
Environment (where), eg I live in London.

Powerful and effective communication is congruent – identity, belief, capability and behaviour are aligned with themselves and with the environment. Marks & Spencer is a good example of a brand that, even without advertising in the conventional sense, has achieved congruent communication – through its PR, shop environments, product ranges, and service, all of which are unified under the name St Michael.

Consumers have received a very consistent message: they understand the *vision* of Marks & Spencer, which is about quality and integrity in retailing; the brand offers access to the consumer who feels it is 'my kind of shop'; its beliefs are clearly stated (eg good quality standards, good value, refunds/returns); the shops offer a range of products which demonstrate its broadening capabilities (clothes, food, plants, home furnishings); the behaviour of both the staff and the products is entirely consonant with the higher levels of communication; finally not only are Marks & Spencer found in the UK, but in France and the US too.

The main point to understand about these levels of communication is that the higher up the scale, the more intimate, the more revealing and the more emotionally loaded the communication. There is a suggestion that the same is true of advertising. A brand communication that is successful at the level of identity (and offers congruency through the other levels) will be more motivating for consumers than a competitive brand in the same market place that is communicating, albeit successfully, at the level of capability.

If the IBM campaign ('I think therefore IBM'), which is pitching its communication at the level of identity, is effective in this task *and* its communication is congruent at the lower levels, then it stands a chance against Apple, which is pitched at the level of capability (the marketing department submits a beautifully presented report in record time).

During the early 1980s, many brand advertisers recognised instinctively the power of communicating at the level of identity, but many failed, through a lack of understanding of how to achieve this form of mass communication. Much of the dreadful lifestyle advertising at this time was unsuccessful in both its branding role ('nice ad, pity I can't remember the product name') and in reflecting the consumer ('they're yuppies, unreal people, not me'). This led to advertisers becoming wary of all 'lifestyle' solutions, perhaps losing an opportunity for an effective identity-level brand communication.

At the tail-end of the 1980s there was a spate of very successful commercials in the UK which communicated the brands' essential identity – K Shoes, VW Polo, Piedmont, Virgin Airlines. All showed an understanding of how to convey the core personality of each brand, that is, its emotional identity, in a way which encouraged consumer identification and involvement, and which helped to differentiate it from its competitors.

Through research it is possible to understand the levels at which a brand and its competitors are communicating, in order to identify whether an opportunity exists to leap-frog the competition and to achieve a congruent, powerful communications strategy for the brand.

Reframing a Negative Brand Image

In recent years, we have seen many brands emerge from what can only be termed 'brand death', to enjoy a new lease of life. Lucozade, Brylcreem, Hovis, and Ribena are a few famous examples. How did Lucozade come out of the sick-room into the arena of athletic energy and well-being? How did Brylcreem become the trendy hair-gel for young men in the 1980s, after disappearing for almost a generation? The answer lies in a process called *Reframing*.

Reframing is a way of changing a negative perception into a positive one by changing the frame of reference used to perceive the experience.

There are two types of reframing: context reframing and content reframing. Context reframing involves taking a brand which seems to be undesirable, and communicating it in another context. Content reframing involves taking the same undesirable brand and reframing what it means to consumers. Two examples come to mind. The pregnancy testing kit, Predictor, was negatively associated with unwanted pregnancies and pre-abortion diagnosis. However, the brand was also bought by women who desperately wanted a child and preferred to test at home rather than repeatedly worrying their GPs. The advertising reframed the brand so that Predictor came to mean something positive.

For the most fantastic news ever in the history of the world.

WHY PREDICTOR IS SO QUICK AND EASY
Unlike many other home pregnancy tests, with Predictor Colourtip you just have a single, simple, one-step test to do.

And because it's simpler, it works faster. In as little as five minutes, WHY PREDICTOR IS RIGHT FIRST TIME Not only is Predictor the easiest test to

use, it's also wonderfully reliable.
In fact, over the last two decades, we've given accurate results to over 50 million women. Predictor Colourtip home pregnancy test.

It's simple, reliable and ... "really incredible."

—PREDICTOR—
RIGHT FIRST TIME

Triumph bras were strongly associated with form and fit – attributes which, although worthy, were associated with frumpiness and lack of contemporary femininity. By advertising the brand in a new way so that form and fit came to mean comfort and naturalness, Triumph – 'the bra for the way you are' became relevant to the style and emotional requirements of women in the late 1980s.

SOLVING BRAND PROBLEMS THROUGH HEIGHTENED AWARENESS

Most brand research, whether qualitative or quantitative, takes place outside the decision-making or purchase context. In viewing rooms or shopping malls around the country and abroad, consumers are asked to describe how they make decisions about brands, what factors influence purchase and how brands are consumed. With the best of goodwill, respondents in research situations cooperate by giving a logical analysis of behaviour. But real life is not like research. At the point of purchase, or even at the point of consumption, consumers are not consciously aware of exactly which stimuli are triggering behaviour, particularly if the behaviour is taken for granted because it has become part of everyday life.

While research can never completely mirror real life, there are strategies that can heighten awareness of real behaviour. The first is artificially to alter habitual behaviour before qualitative interviewing takes place.

In a study on a brand of toilet cleaner, respondents were requested not to clean their toilets for a week prior to the research. The majority were unable to proceed with the experiment for the full period, because the discomfort generated was so extreme! However the experience heightened awareness of the emotional feelings attached to toilet cleaning, and specifically those attached to the brand used regularly. In a study designed to understand the meaning of milk, respondents were asked to forego milk, in any form at all, for a week prior to the research. By the time they arrived at the group discussion, respondents were panting for a cup of tea or coffee! The task had also heightened awareness of how the typical English breakfast of bacon and/or eggs has become replaced by cereal and milk for the family. All kinds of foods had suddenly vanished from the shopping list – cheese, yoghurt, ready-to-eat desserts, ice-cream, sauces and soups. The exercise led to an increased awareness of the strength of consumer belief in the versatility and bone-building values of milk.

Another method of heightening behavioural awareness is 'accompanied shopping' – a form of participant observation. A respondent is accompanied by a researcher as she engages in a task – choosing wallpaper, selecting a lounge suite, deciding on a vacuum cleaner, shopping for clothes, buying food in a supermarket. The researcher informs the respondent (or couple, eg husband/wife, best friends, mother/daughter) that her role is to observe the behaviour of the staff, the way the merchandise is arranged, the speed of access, but she is in fact observing how the respondent behaves in-store, particularly the point-of-sale features to which the respondent pays attention, and her behaviour with regard to the brand in question. Afterwards, the researcher and respondent(s) spend time in a more conventional interview, exploring behaviour of which either or both has become aware.

To conclude this chapter, I would like to end with the visualisation that a brand is like a diamond – no two are exactly the same except to the untutored eye. If you consult with an expert who encourages you to look through his special magnifying glass at each facet in turn, pointing out flaws, colour variance and size differences, you will know and understand the true value of your diamond. So too with brands. By examining each facet of your brand in relation to its competitors under the guidance of an expert using the tools of qualitative and quantitative approaches developed for brands, you too can discover the true value of your brand. If it is found to lack worth, you will also know how to recut it so that you obtain the best value possible.

CHAPTER THREE

Brands and the Role of Advertising

GARY DUCKWORTH

Gary Duckworth has spent fifteen years in the advertising business, starting at BMP, followed by six years at Abbott, Mead, Vickers where he was a board director. In 1989 he left his post as head of planning at HDM/Horner Collis Kirvan to become a founder partner of Duckworth, Finn, Grubb, Waters. DFGW's early success has been built on attracting major brand names, including Prudential, Duckhams and Melitta.

He is a member of the IPA and involved in a number of their courses, as well as sitting on their Education and Training Committee. He was deputy chairman of the APG in 1989/90 and has spoken on advertising and planning issues to a variety of audiences, in the UK, Europe and Japan.

Brands and the Role of Advertising

G A R Y   D U C K W O R T H

THE FIRST SHAPES OF EXPERIENCE

When a human being is born it starts out with an unshaped and unstructured consciousness. Think for a moment of how the world appears to a new human being. A new-born baby doesn't focus on its surroundings. It can tell the difference between light and dark. It has a primitive sense of touch. It can taste, it can feel hunger and it can feel pain. The world of a new baby is a world of vague sensations, of events which it makes no sense of.

Amid the confusion of all the stimuli of the experiences around it, it learns as it grows to begin to make a kind of sense of the shapes and sensations that envelop it. Out of the chaos of disparate elements its consciousness begins to create patterns, groups, collectivities of sensations.

These collectivities form entities in a baby's mind. As child psychologists tell us, a baby first learns to recognise its mother. Not, of course, in the way that we as adults recognise our own mothers. A baby's first experience of its mother is a collection of impressions:

- a vague shape
- the tone of her voice
- perhaps the sound of a familiar and repeated word – maybe its own name.

A baby first learns to recognise its mother when it puts together this vague collection of sounds and sensations into some kind of coherent entity. So when this entity approaches and picks it up, it is calmed, it stops crying, it goes to sleep. And as its capacity to make noises develops, a baby's parents take the primitive incoherent noises that it makes, and start to shape its conscious mind so that it learns to give them a name.

'Mama'

Names like 'mama' or 'dada' are the names that we learn for the fundamental collections of sensations that shape the infant consciousness.

It is precisely this power of the human mind to associate experiences – to gather them together and group them under a name – that enables us to bring pattern, order and shape to the world.

Creating Meaning out of Chaos

In one word, this ability to associate enables us to create *meaning* – meaning out of chaos. As we grow, we learn to give names to objects and their meanings: 'apple', 'dentist', 'school', 'ice-cream', 'Esther Rantzen'.

These names certainly refer to these objects, but they also have a far broader function in our lives. 'Ice-cream' becomes associated with a pleasurable set of tastes and sensations, of flavours, maybe certain times of day, or when a child has been behaving well. Conversely, 'dentist' in my childhood, before the days of painless dentistry, was associated with pain, with the smell of the methylated spirits used to sterilise instruments.

So through our experience of life we learn not just the names of things, but also whole sets of associations that become connected and fastened. These associations are learnt in various contexts – in school, at home with our families, at the dentists, in adolescence – and so on.

The society we live in and the upbringing we have creates the meanings in our lives. So the meanings we gather and carry around with us are a function of social interaction, of social relationships. Over time, the meanings that we attach to these named entities can often change, as new associations supplant old ones. For example, the name 'dentist' for me no longer holds the terrors it once did.

Sometimes we deliberately change the names we use, to show to ourselves or the outside world that our relationship with a name has changed. Consider the difference between 'daddy' and 'dad'. A growing child learns to use the word 'dad' to indicate to the outside world that it is growing up, that things have changed.

SOCIAL MEANINGS – THE MIRROR AND THE CAT

As we grow up we become socialised into the particular society and time that we have been born into. We learn that objects have social meanings as well as functional attributes.

The Egyptians thought all cats were divine. They worshipped them. We don't worship cats today – their social meaning has changed, though the creatures themselves are still more or less the same.

In the fourteenth and fifteenth centuries, to have a mirror in your house had a social meaning of immense affluence, because the technology of making mirrors had only just been invented – it was very difficult and very expensive. That's why in this fifteenth century picture by van Eyck, the Arnolfinis were painted with a mirror in the background.

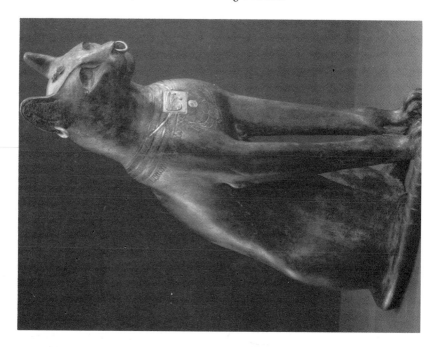

Van Eyck, *The Arnolfini Marriage*

Of course, to us today the presence of mirrors in such paintings, unless we are students of art history, would not give us these meanings – because the social meaning of the mirror has changed. But note that only the social meaning has changed – we still use the object in functional terms in more or less the same way they did five hundred years ago.

The Mercedes Coupé and the Sedan Chair

In seventeenth-century London, the wife of a rich man would travel around in a sedan chair – he usually had a carriage. The sedan chair was the social equivalent of the car for the wife of the man who has everything. Today, one of those small Mercedes coupés has probably the same social meaning.

The sedan chair

The Mercedes coupé

These meanings that we attach to the objects of the material world are not just something that we carry internally, but are fundamental in determining our relationship with the outside world.

The picture I've built so far is one where human beings, through the associative power of the human mind, learn to give names to the objects of the world around us, and then have the ability to connect meanings to them, meanings that we learn from the social framework in which we live. And in this process we also learn to use and exploit these meanings to say things about ourselves. We float in a sea of meanings, significations and signs, and it is our arrangement of these which shapes the world as we see it, and which structures and guides our behaviour. The world we look out on is the world we have learnt to arrange.

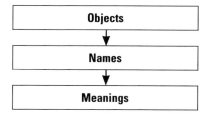

The creation of meaning

THE CONNECTION WITH BRANDS

As western societies moved through industrialisation into the developed capitalism of the late nineteenth century, they started to manufacture consumer products which met the needs of the growing and affluent Victorian middle class.

The manufacturers had business needs – to build their sales and to sell goods profitably. In order to do this they had to find consumers – to build a stable and predictable consumer demand for their output. In other words they had to create loyal consumer relationships, so that people would return over and over again to buy their products.

As new consumer markets emerged, the capacity of human beings to associate and carry meanings, and to attach them to objects with names, was exploited by manufacturers, and there developed the use of the brand, or more particularly the brand name.

The brand name at this stage was used for simple everyday household and personal items: Bird's custard powder, Rowland's macassar oil, Cadbury's cocoa. From the consumer's point of view, it was a manufacturer's sign, denoting a particular product so that when they, or their servants, shopped they would know what product to buy to meet a particular need. But the brand name also functioned as an endorsement, indicating not just authenticity, but also a guarantee of quality or consistency of performance.

This enabled consumers to simplify and structure their buying patterns as consumer manufacturing developed, because they learnt to associate these brand names with a set of meanings by which they could clearly identify the products that met their needs. So that when they had a need, like for starched collars, or a hot condiment to flavour food, they knew to ask for Robin starch or Colman's mustard.

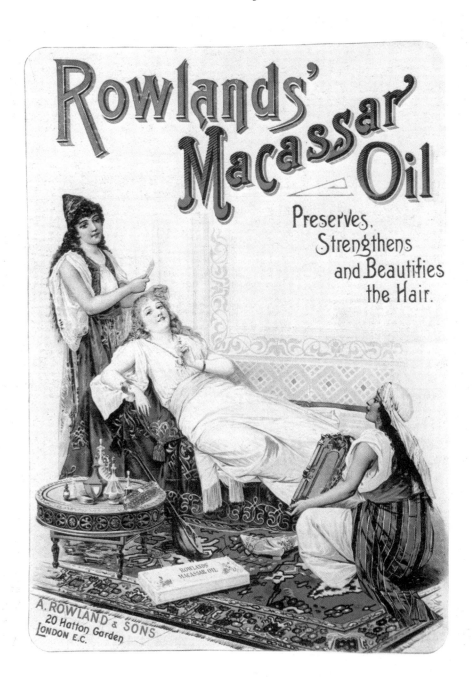

And as consumers learned to become loyal to particular brands because they delivered product benefits successfully, manufacturers created stable patterned relationships with the people who bought their products. Relationships like preference, like 'always buy', like 'prepared to pay more for' – all the kinds of vital continuities that were essential if mass manufacturing was to survive and prosper.

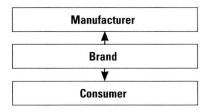

The dual role of the brand

Modern-day Brands

Essentially the role of the brand in our society today is no different. Just as a baby learns to make sense of its own world by attaching names and meanings to experiences, so brands enable us to make sense and to create meanings for ourselves in the social world of consumption in which *we* participate.

Imagine, for example, if we took someone from a culture completely different from our own – maybe from an Amazonian tribe – and set them down in a supermarket here – the experience of seeing all the packets on the shelves would be completely meaningless – they simply couldn't make sense of it. For us, however, packaging carries meanings, significations and signs which enable us to move quickly through the shopping process, satisfying our needs:

- not just for coffee, but for ground coffee taste without the grind;
- not just for soap, but for a little touch of luxury every day;
- not just for sauce, but for the authentic experience of Italian food.

These are the brands that manufacturers have created to meet the needs of our lives, and these are the meanings that we, in our culture and times have learnt to attach to them.

THE ROLE OF BRAND ADVERTISING

Once you understand a brand as a collection of meanings commonly held by human beings, and that these meanings affect people's purchasing behaviour, the part that advertising can play in the fortunes of a brand becomes clear. The role of advertising is to manipulate the meanings connected with the brand to the brand owner's advantage. *Advertising manipulates the meaning of brands.*

This may sound a little strange at first, but it helps to clear up a lot of the basic misconceptions that emerge when we talk about advertising – the simplistic idea, for example, that advertising is there 'to sell' – well, yes, of course it is, but for people who are involved in the development of brand campaigns, this kind of notion doesn't get us very far because it doesn't explain *how* it does it.

Much of what advertising does is to create the forcible evolution of the meanings that are attached to a brand. Brands swim around in the same kind of social soup that we all swim around in. And as the ingredients of that soup change, so brands have to change their flavour.

What advertising does is to equip us with new lenses with which to look at products, as our own social outlook and the times we live in change, so that purchasing those products from a particular brand name continues to make sense to us, and these products continue to occupy a relevant space in our lives. And thus brand owners maintain long-term relationships with their customers, and provide long-term stability for their businesses.

Advertising as Intervention

We need to take the argument one step further. We need a framework to understand how and why a campaign manipulates a brand's meaning in a particular case.

To provide this framework it is helpful to bring in a concept from the world of medicine. When a surgeon performs an operation, for example to cure a patient suffering from the symptoms of heart disease, he makes an *intervention*. The intervention is *specific* – ie it takes into account the patient's specific problem, for example removing an arterial blockage – and it is also *directional* – it has an objective in mind, to arrest the course of the disease.

In exactly the same way, when we are considering how a particular campaign works, we can also think of it as an intervention – something which actively *intervenes* in the brand—user relationship. And for this intervention to be effective and of value it has to be:

- *Specific* to the particular circumstances of the brand – the needs of the people in the market in which it operates, its history, its competitors, the meanings which have become attached to it during the course of its life.

- *Directional* – it seeks to achieve something on behalf of the brand owner. So it must emerge from the brand owner's objectives – their business needs which determine the kind of consumer relationships they want to develop. For example, to recruit new users to the brand, or to maintain the loyalty of current users in the face of competitive attack.

Oxo and Lucozade: Changing the Lenses we Look Through

Oxo and Lucozade are two classic examples of brands which have been sustained and evolved through the decades. Both are examples where the underlying product itself has remained virtually unchanged, while advertising has played a pivotal role in evolving their meanings so that they continue to enjoy strong, continuous consumer relationships.

Since the Katie and Philip campaign of the 1960s, the Oxo cube has been portrayed as playing a central role in the creation of satisfying meals. In addition to its functional role in meal enhancement, the brand has had emotional meanings attached to it: it has been associated with the reward that comes from preparing a meal that people appreciate. These emotional meanings are all important: by building emotional ties the brand gains strengthened relationships with its users, which enable it to maintain a healthy position, *vis à vis* competitive products. And although rival manufacturers have launched challenges to Oxo's supremacy, none have proved successful in undermining the popularity of the brand with its users.

In the latest advertising intervention in the life of the Oxo brand, we can see the specific and directional characteristics at work. As society has evolved, meal repertoires and family life have changed: Oxo is now shown contributing to a wide variety of dishes, including vegetarian ones, and the social context in which the brand is depicted has evolved from the somewhat idealised 'perfect housewife' style of the Katie campaign to the current 'ordinary warts-and-all family'. By evolving these aspects of the brand's meanings, advertising has enabled it to retain its place in the midst of culinary and social change, and to build relationships with new users, people who were not even born when the Katie campaign emerged. And while these meanings have shifted, the meanings of 'meal enhancement' and 'emotional reward' have remained central – they are merely expressed in a different way.

In many respects, therefore, it is more useful to think of brands as constantly evolving phenomena, rather than being in any sense

The evolution of Oxo

fixed. So a useful model is to think of brands as having a kind of atomic structure, in which the nucleus of the brand is composed of those meanings that tend to remain relatively unchanged over time, while the meanings orbiting around the nucleus can fade, or be added to through advertising interventions.

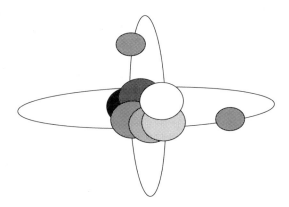

Brands: an atomic structure

The history of Lucozade is a fascinating example of how advertising intervention, by modifying the meanings of the brand, has played a part in enabling it to create relationships with entirely different sets of users over time, thus ensuring the brand's survival.

In the late 1970s the Lucozade brand had very clear associations – as an aid to recovery from sickness, for children, and therefore for occasional use. The brand's user base was declining because the population was becoming healthier in the longer term, and thus the number of occasions in which the brand's primary meaning became relevant were also declining. The purpose of advertising intervention was to create more regular purchase. Analysis of how the brand was actually *used* (ie the brand's *specific* circumstances) showed that a large proportion of its volume came from adult drinking as a refreshing drink or pick-me-up, and was not sickness-related.

The advertising evolved new meanings for the brand, this time seeking to strengthen relationships with the adult target group – active, health-concerned women – by retaining the core 'energy-giving' meaning of the brand, but putting it in the context of more frequent, everyday 'in health' usage. By associating the brand with this new usage, the volume decline was reversed, while the product itself and the packaging remained unchanged.

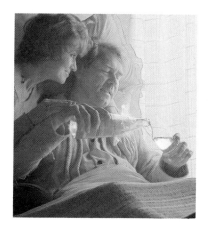

The evolution of Lucozade

Latterly advertising intervention, in conjunction with packaging and distribution extension, has taken the core 'energy-giving' meaning, and associated the brand with physical achievement and sporting success. This has created relationships with young adults, so that Lucozade now competes very successfully as well in the teenage soft drinks market.

CREATING AND EVALUATING BRAND ADVERTISING

The Oxo and Lucozade examples both show how advertising intervention emerges out of the specific circumstances of the brand, and the way each campaign has a particular direction which relates to the brand owner's needs. Both take the product which lies at the heart of the brand and then 'wrap' it in some contemporary social meanings which give it a significance and a clear role in the lives of the target group.

The *specific* nature of brand advertising is a very important point to grasp – *there can be no 'all-purpose' general rule for developing advertising campaigns, which fits all brands in all circumstances* – each intervention must be specific to the brand and the brand owner's needs at the time.

Hence, although many people both in the advertising business and outside it have tried to build formulae, ie all-purpose models of campaign construction and advertising 'measurement', they have failed because the more abstract and all-purpose they become, the more they lack the ability to be situation and brand-specific. It's as if we invented a vegetable evaluation machine, and tomatoes, aubergines, onions and cabbage were judged with respect to the same criteria – presence of seeds, red colour, strong smell etc – without regard to their culinary role and function. When we create a campaign we are creating a bespoke item. There is no Big Mac in advertising.

Building the Case

So what's the starting point for developing a campaign for a brand?

It has to start with a process of *interrogation* – a process of asking relevant questions to build a picture of 'what is going on' in the broadest sense between the brand and its current or potential users. This process is an *iterative* one, where the answer to each question raises yet more questions or avenues for investigation, and the picture of 'what is going on' is built up from a variety of 'clues', in much the same way that a detective works out who committed a murder – from following up witnesses, backing hunches, eliminating red herrings, and using his knowledge and experience of human motivation and need to build an overall scheme of events. Advertising, like crime, is a very human thing: if we seek to use it to influence people's behaviour, an understanding of human motivation and 'what makes people tick' is of as much value to us as it is to a detective.

During this process the investigation is framed by some basic but important rules of how markets work:

- The 80:20 rule, whereby typically 80 per cent of sales in a market are accounted for by 20 per cent of the users who create the market.
- The fact that if we are to increase a brand's sales, in user terms there are only two basic ways this can happen:
  - by getting more people to use the brand (increasing penetration)
  - by getting existing users to use it more often (increasing frequency);

or both.

We then start asking the 'big' questions, for example:

- The overall fortunes of the market – is it growing or declining because consumers are entering or exiting?
- Is the product still appropriate for the needs of the users in the market – is it packaged in such a way that it expresses the meanings we want?
- Are sales or market share increasing or declining – and why?
- Is share declining because competitors are usurping the brand's place in its users' repertoires, so the brand is bought less frequently, or are people actually deserting the brand?
- Has the brand's price changed relative to its competitors?
- What are the effects of distribution on the brand's progress?

The investigative angle needs to be a dynamic one: we need to understand where and why the brand is moving. Markets rarely, if ever stand still, especially these days. If the nature of advertising intervention is to be dynamic and so to create some kind of movement, we have to understand the eddies and swirls of consumer behaviour that our brand is already subject to.

At this early stage of the interrogation, the emphasis is on trying to provide some kind of numbers-based 'macro' framework for examining the brand's circumstances, in which the basic problem is defined.

Although the information is simple, it is at this stage that we usually start to form some picture of the user relationships the brand enjoys, and the patterns they fall into.

If we use the first stage to identify the broad 'macro' patterns and the groups of people who are of interest to us, the next stage is used to get much closer to the brand and its role in the lives and purchasing repertoires of these people.

Ordinarily this stage uses qualitative research. There is nothing special or mystical about qualitative research, though sometimes its practitioners portray it as such. If we recognise that brands exist in the minds of human beings, and are created from the circumstances of consumption in their everyday lives, qualitative research enables us to 'take a bath' in the *human* context in which the brand exists. (It's a slightly strange thought, but future social historians may well find some of the richest understanding of our times through reading the reports of qualitative studies of brands and their role in people's lives. No age has ever been better documented in terms of the minutiae and the everyday perceptions of the lives of ordinary people.)

Qualitative research at this second stage is a directional process, and is framed by the questions that have emerged earlier: we can use it to ask questions about fairly rational, straightforward things like purchasing repertoires, and how products are used. But *its fundamental value is that it enables us to investigate in depth the associations a brand has and where these meanings have come from:* the product itself, its packaging, the social context in which it is used, its previous advertising and so on.

From the consumer's point of view, of course, the brand appears as a totality – the meanings it has acquired will be blended together into an interrelated whole. It is part of the qualitative investigation to unravel these interrelationships and understand how the construction of meanings has taken place.

By integrating our picture of the consumers we want to develop relationships with, together with our understanding of how the brand has developed its existing relationships, we can see if and how the brand's meaning requires modification, and it is this which provides us with the starting point for understanding the role that advertising intervention needs to take:

- What meanings does it have now?
- What meanings does it need to have to create the relationships we need?

Of course, it may be that other forms of marketing intervention are required *as well as advertising* – a new packaging format or distribution growth – to complete the necessary changes so that all the new relationships we need can arise.

SOCIAL DEVELOPMENT AND THE NEW TYPES OF BRAND

As society changes, new types of businesses grow big and financially powerful, due to changes in the underlying economic and social structure. The primary underlying cause of the long-term growth which is happening in the advertising market in the UK is that new types of brand owner have come to advertising agencies to develop new and additional meanings for themselves, in order to exert greater leverage for themselves in people's lives, and to compete with each other more effectively.

The last twenty years have seen the growth of massive new advertising categories – cars, retailers, corporations, airlines, banks, to name only some. The result is that the owners of these new types of brand now appear to occupy a much larger role in the perceptual world we inhabit. They in their turn have become part of the flavour of the age. Just as in some respects the 1960s 'means' the age of Daz and Fry's chocolate, so the 1980s were in some way defined by the arrival of Vector and Next.

As new categories of brand owner come to the fore, their brands become part of the very fabric and experience of our age. And the arrival of these new categories of brand has given us new challenges, because in some very important respects they're very different from the product-based brands that preceded them.

Meanings and the Power of Experience

Take a retailer, and look at how people create meanings when they go into a store. There's the merchandise, the range of goods on offer, the price. They attach all kinds of meanings to the store brand name just from their experience of these aspects alone. But there's also the interior look and feel of the place, the way things are laid out, there's the attitude and behaviour of the staff. People in a store get involved with the merchandise – they touch it, feel it, inspect it.

Similar things apply in a bank – we walk inside it, it is designed in a certain way, we deal with the people at the counter, we form opinions about their attitude to us, the bank sends us letters and statements, occasionally we see the manager.

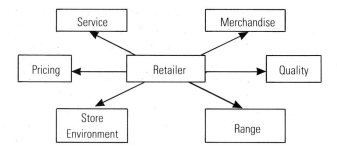

Retailers – multifaceted brands

What characterises these brands is first, they are more *complex*, precisely because they are multifaceted. And second, we have a much more *involved* and *interactive* experience with these types of brand, and they present a whole new set of challenges, if we are to analyse and understand the role advertising can play.

First, because these brands are more complex, they are more difficult to analyse. Second, the meanings of this kind of brand are much more heavily anchored in our direct experience of the world – because our experience of them is so much more involved.

Let's take an example. Consider the question 'What is the difference between a supermarket and a commodity lager in terms of how their meanings are derived?' If we could quantify the sum total of the meanings each of them has, the proportion deriving from advertising versus that from direct experience would be very different.

Lagers vs. Supermarket – Where do Meanings Come From?

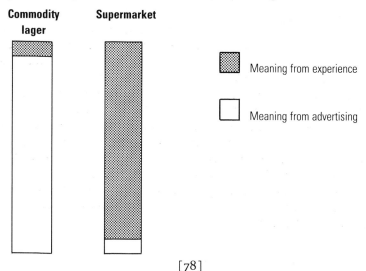

In the case of a lager brand, probably something like 95 per cent of the meaning of the brand is advertising-created. People often say the advertising *is* the brand. And they're quite correct. But what's interesting is *why* they're right. They're right because the experiential contribution of drinking a commodity lager is pretty unstimulating. It doesn't in itself create much meaning – it's not as rich or as multifaceted an experience as walking round a store.

That's why retailers like M & S or Paul Smith can create really powerful brand images with virtually no advertising at all. The idea of creating a meaningful lager brand without advertising to supply meanings is unthinkable.

ADVERTISING AND EXPERIENTIAL BRANDS

The role advertising can play with brands like these has to be worked out very carefully, because of this experiential element. If a bank gives lousy service, there's no point in advertising that the bank really cares about good service when the experience of people going there is telling them loud and clear that it doesn't.

There have been major examples of attempts to shift brand meanings which have failed because the experience of the brand inhibited the ability of the advertising to attach new meanings – 'This is the age of the train,' and 'That's the wonder of Woolworths' are both examples of campaigns that failed because they could not outweigh the power of experience.

So what can advertising do for brands like these? What it can do is draw attention to those positive aspects of our experience that the brand *does* deliver, and by heightening our perception of these, help us forget or at least pay less attention to the less appealing aspects of the brand's performance. Consider the InterCity campaign.

The campaign focused on the relaxing aspects of InterCity travel (not 'British Rail' travel). The campaign did not talk about arriving on time, or the pleasant service we could expect from the staff. It talked about a facet of our experience that *does* tend to be confirmed by rail travel. By using the brand name 'InterCity' and attaching 'relaxing travel experience' meanings to it, advertising intervened to create a brand out of a small part of our total experience of what 'British Rail' means, and thus enabled British Rail to compete more effectively with the car for inter-city journeys.

InterCity – 'relax'

With service-oriented companies, where the quality of service provided to the customer is an important part of the brand meaning, the role of advertising intervention is as much *internal* as it is external, because the advertising defines for the staff of the company what it means to work for that company, as much as it defines for the customer what it means to be on the receiving end of that service. Advertising is frequently used in this way when a service company seeks to motivate its staff to new levels of commitment and delivery. So with this kind of brand the advertising is again employed to build relationships, but this time by defining a whole set of roles and expectations between customers and the staff of the company. British Airways is one of the best examples in recent years.

CONCLUSION

What I hope I've put across is that although brands and brand advertising are relatively recent phenomena in the scale of human history, the underlying mechanisms of the way they work are dependent on human characteristics which have always existed. And if we seek to create and evolve powerful brands through advertising, there is no substitute for creative insight and understanding of the human society in which we live.

CHAPTER FOUR

Media Planning to Build Brands

KEN NEW

Ken New joined the advertising business in 1965, working with CPV, Hobson Bates and McCann Erickson before joining French Gold Abbott as media director, when he first worked with David Abbott.

After three years as media director of French Gold Abbott, he moved across to become an account director for a further two years – a sabbatical in account management!

Ken joined AMV as media director in 1978 when David Abbott, Peter Mead and Adrian Vickers set up the agency, and he was recently appointed vice-chairman of the agency.

He is the current chairman of the Advertising Association Media Business Course, a member of the Media Circle Council, and past member of the IPA Media Policy Group.

Media Planning to Build Brands

KEN NEW

'The medium is the message', wrote Marshall McLuhan, his premise being that the form of the medium is a far more powerful influence than the content of the medium, in determining what is being communicated.

But, of course, there is the counter-argument. The medium is but a vehicle. It carries a message. It is the message that matters.

Clearly, the truth lies somewhere between the two. However, it is difficult to argue that, in the communication of brand values and brand properties, it is not the message (in advertising terms, the creative message) that is the most important element in the mix. Indeed, should it not be the first objective of every media proposal to give the creative message 'centre stage'; to give the creative message the best possible chance of working?

To achieve that requires an understanding (or, in the absence of an understanding, at least a point of view) of the extent to which a medium can enhance or diminish the effectiveness of a piece of communication and, as importantly, the standing of a brand featured in that communication. Or, put another way, an understanding of 'media effect'.

That there is such a phenomenon as 'media effect' is in little doubt. That it is clearly understood is in some doubt. That there are firmly-held opinions about it is in no doubt.

Media effect is not something that can be easily be measured. However, that, in itself, should not be allowed to relegate it in importance:

'Atmosphere, context and impact. These three words, once so important in media planning, have become less popular largely because of the difficulty of measuring them.'
(James R Adams, Media Planning, 1971)

'There is a general belief that, in advertising, the medium is at least part of the messsage, more specifically that the environment provided by the medium can be a considerable help or hindrance to the effectiveness of advertising. There are a whole range of strongly held attitudes about newspapers, magazines and television which might affect attitudes to brands advertised through them. For media types, at least, the lack of evidence seems attributable not so much to attitude transfer not occurring, as to the difficulties involved in establishing that it does.'
(*J Nolan, Combined Media Campaigns, Thomsons Awards 1969*)

'We all know – don't we – that the medium is part of the message. We believe that the surroundings of an advertisement affect the way in which it convinces – or not – the reader of its sales argument. This belief has been shrouded in mystery by the inability (or apparent inability) to measure it to any quantifiable degree.
(*Alan Copage, Magazine Marketplace, Spring 1984*)

'To some extent 'character' (eg size, audience) can be measured by external means such as research, and in years to come the extent of this measurement may well be widened; but the effect of atmosphere will always be largely a matter of common sense and informed perception.'
(*John Hobson, The Selection of Advertising Media, 1955*)

It is not the intent, nor would it be possible, in this chapter to provide the definitive statement on media effect – decades of effort by leading academics have failed to achieve that. The aim of the chapter is fourfold, namely:

1. to discuss some of the accepted wisdom of our industry – accepted wisdom that is applied every day of our working lives and upon which major brand-support decisions are based;
2. to attempt to throw some light on consumer attitudes to brands in the context of the medium in which they appear;
3. to summarise some of the findings of published research on the subject of 'media effect';
4. to draw some conclusions on the extent, nature and importance of media effect on brand perceptions.

ACCEPTED WISDOM

Listen to anybody involved in the development and deployment of advertising and he or she will, without exception, express a point of view about media effect. It could be a point of view between media types (eg television vs. magazines) or within media types (eg *Womans Own* vs. *Vogue*). It will tend to be a point of view based on three things:

- What the medium has to offer in terms of its characteristics (eg television offers the opportunity to use picture, sound and movement).
- What the medium has been seen to achieve in the past (experience).
- The perceived relationship between the medium and its audience.

At this stage, it is worth looking at some of the accepted wisdom surrounding media effect. It is by no means an exhaustive listing. But what is interesting about many of the views listed below is how widely they are accepted, and the conviction with which they are held.

TELEVISION

Television, probably more than any other medium, benefits from accepted wisdom. Much of its standing is derived from the fact that it has been seen to work. It has been responsible for building brands and for changing brand perceptions. (Or would it be more correct to say that it has the characteristics to allow the development of a particular piece of communication – and it is the piece of communication that has influenced the brand perceptions?)

We are told in advertising textbooks that 'nothing can create a brand image more dramatically or sell more persuasively than film, with its use of such elements as music, emotion, humour, animation and personalities.' Couple this with the public's appreciation – and the public of the 1990s is remarkably 'media aware' – of the scale and cost of television, then it is no surprise that it is held in such high esteem:

> 'I believe that television does give a brand status and scale... by merely appearing on television a brand can appropriate some of the authoritative attributes of the medium... people regard television as an advertising medium with a degree of "awe" and that anybody advertising on it must be "special"... people feel that advertising on television is very expensive and that anybody using the medium must have resource.'
> *(Alec Kenny, Managing Partner, Kenny, Lockett, Booth)*

'Television provides brands with a pedigree and status because of its perceived "size" and acknowledged impact/effectiveness.'
(John Ayling, Managing Director, John Ayling Associates)

'There are many examples of advertisers who have gained by "trading up" in their choice of media. There is, undoubtedly, a pecking order between the media – and television is top.'
(Nick Horswell, PHD)

A telling illustration of the perceived importance of *being seen to be* on television appeared in an advertisement for Club Riviera, a timeshare company, which appeared in the 27 March 1990 edition of *The Daily Express*, (the time at which this chapter was being written). The reputation of all timeshare companies has clearly been sullied by the widely publicised, and unacceptable, practices of the few. (Indeed, the timeshare industry has been the subject of a recent public enquiry.)

In order to reassure potential customers of their reputation and reliability, Club Riviera set aside a significant proportion of the advertisement to list their credentials. But, just in case the reader still wasn't totally reassured, in a banner across the whole advertisement were splashed the words 'AS ADVERTISED ON TV!!'

An interesting irony. Despite the standing of a major national newspaper, this particular advertiser still felt the need to use the television medium as a means of brand reassurance.

However, there is perhaps, for some brands, a downside to television. It is a very 'public' medium, a medium watched by everybody. Therefore, if exclusivity is an important element of a brand's appeal, could it not be argued that its use as a support medium might have a detrimental effect on the brand's image? 'If it's on television, it can't be that exclusive – everybody watches television.'

Experience suggests that if exclusivity, prestige or esteem are key ingredients of a brand property, then television – or, more specifically, the medium of film – is more than capable of being used to communicate them – indeed, develop them.

When American Express chose to use television to accelerate its business growth, it was a case of a mass medium being used for what was a deliberately elitist product. Michael Baulk described the American Express 'That will do nicely' campaign as:

'... an educative campaign. It set out to explain what the chargecard is, how you use it and how convenient it is. But those basic logical messages were package wrapped in high status, high snob-appeal, elitist advertising.'

American Express is one of many television campaigns to have demonstrated that it is the content, style and the tone of the advertising that matters. The effect of the medium itself will, at best, be positive and, at worst, be neutral.

Within the television medium, opinions on the effect of station or programme environment are less firm. There is research evidence that suggests that viewers watch programmes, not stations. However, this may change as dedicated stations (eg sports stations, music stations) establish themselves.

There is research evidence that suggests that a direct relationship exists between programme interest and programme/commercial attention – indeed, even likelihood to purchase. There is, however, no evidence to suggest that commercials work any harder, or that brands are perceived any differently, when featured in one programme or another. This is a matter of judgement for the television buyer.

I believe that programme environment does matter. The tone, style, character and content of a programme have a direct bearing, not just on the number and type of people it attracts, but on their state of mind, their mood and their relationship with that programme – and, in turn, the manner in which the commercials and brands within that programme are received and perceived. *Coronation*

Street may well generate as many ABC1 ratings as *News at Ten*, but would a commercial for Hanson Trust or *The Independent* work as hard in that environment?

And importantly, as more and more dedicated television channels segment the audience into special interest groups, so the influence and importance of programme environment will increase:

> 'It may well be that the viewer to a music channel will feel that any commercial on that channel is "for me" and will treat that with an interest that they might not on a channel which has to appeal to everybody.'
> *(Alec Kenny, Managing Partner, Kenny, Lockett, Booth)*

As new television broadcasters segment audiences, so programme-based buying strategies will become more important. Measurement and evaluation will almost certainly become more difficult, but that should not be allowed to detract from what is best for the brand.

OUTDOOR

Outdoor, because of its physical characteristics, also benefits from perceptions of size and scale. Posters are larger than life. Outdoor is a very public medium. The use of the larger roadside sizes (48 sheets and 96 sheets) is a way of making a statement about confidence and resource.

> 'They must be a big company if they can afford to use all those enormous posters.'

> 'They're obviously very confident, because they're being so bold and public about their products.'

Although it is in the area of size, scale and confidence that the media effect of outdoor is normally discussed, the medium is made up of many more smaller site sizes.

Red Stripe is an interesting case, where media effect played an important part in the selection of the type of outdoor support used. But, unlike most advertisers who seek the benefits of scale and widespread presence that outdoor provides, Red Stripe went to the other extreme – fly-posters!

Red Stripe commands a cult status among its users, a status that could well be eroded by insensitive use of media. Fly-posters were the perfect fit. They put the brand at 'street level', among the concert and record announcements. They are an 'unofficial' poster medium, a young people's medium and an urban medium. Fly-posters reflected, precisely, (and probably contributed to) the brand image that Red Stripe wished to communicate. They helped give it 'street cred'.

An effective, if unconventional, interpretation of media effect.

Red Stripe . . . underlining its status as a cult lager

RADIO

Radio probably benefits less than any other medium from positive accepted wisdom. Without doubt, it has suffered a real perception problem throughout the industry:

'I know it gets customers through the door, but can it really build brands?'

'It's a secondary medium. It doesn't have the status or standing of other major media.'

These are typical of advertising industry attitudes towards radio. They are held for a number of reasons.

In part, it's because round-the-clock commercial radio is a relatively new medium to the UK. (If anything that's nearly twenty years old can be described as new!) In part, it's because the medium has, in the past, been both sold and used as a fast, low-cost medium.

Very few companies have got to grips with the real potential of commercial radio and, hence, it has never really built up, through use and experience, a bank of positive, popular perceptions. Accepted wisdom, when it cannot be supported by hard data (as it cannot in most cases) depends upon the confidence of the advocate. Radio has yet to gain that confidence in large pockets of the industry.

However, commercial radio is currently developing, relatively speaking, at a faster rate than any other medium. And the developments, particularly where special interest stations (news/information, jazz, easy listening), community stations and ethnic stations are concerned, will generate a whole new set of listener-station relationships. It is then that media effect will begin to be seriously attributed to the medium.

This, coupled with the portfolio of 'brand' case histories that the medium is building up means that when subsequent editions of this book are published, radio will, undoubtedly, be thought of as much more than just a very effective retail medium (conventional wisdom!)

PRESS

It is in the press medium that accepted wisdom (some might describe it as prejudice), related to media effect, comes to the fore. This is not surprising, because the reader of a publication has *chosen* to look at or read that particular medium, or parts of it, rather than having had it imposed upon him or her.

Readers are more discerning and selective in their choice of reading than viewers in their viewing or listeners in their listening. There are three main reasons for this:

- the number of choices within the medium are much greater
- the differences between the choices are more extreme
- the readers have much more control over the medium in their hands than do the viewers of television or the listeners of radio.

(It will be interesting to examine this situation during the mid/late 1990s and beyond, when viewers will have a greater choice of dedicated stations and channels in both television and radio. Will their access to the broadcast media follow much the same pattern as their access to the press media in their search for news, information, entertainment and special interests?)

The extent of 'accepted wisdom' as it applies to media effect in the press relates to three things:

- the image of a publication (or group of publications)
- the perceived relationship between the publication and its readers
- the empathy or relevance of a brand to the publication's environment.

FINANCIAL TIMES

FT No. 31,449 — THE FINANCIAL TIMES LIMITED 1991   Friday May 10 1991   55p

Yugoslavia gives army wide powers to avert civil war

By Laura Silber in Belgrade

Weekend FT

Tomorrow: The war and its aftermath have barely dented the émigré luxury many Kuwaitis enjoy

Is a mortgage-rate battle looming?

WORLD NEWS

Progress on South African peace talks

Talks between the South African government and the African National Congress have resulted in outline agreement on measures to end the violence in black townships which has left nearly 10,000 people dead since 1984.

The agreement, still to be finalised, involves a ban on the carrying of traditional weapons in public, which the rival black group Inkatha says is required by Zulu culture. South African president Mr F. W. de Klerk appears to have forced the Zulu leader, Chief Mangosuthu Buthelezi, to agree that the carrying of such weapons, apart from spears, should be banned. Page 16

Brazilian ministers quit

A second Brazilian government member, infrastructure minister Eduardo Teixeira, resigned yesterday, hours after economy minister Zelia Cardoso de Mello quit with her team. Page 3; From conflict to consensus, Page 3

June poll denied

Senior Conservatives sought to quell speculation that prime minister John Major is considering a June general election. Colleagues said his sights were set on the autumn. Page 16

Ulster talks deadlocked

Talks on the political future of Northern Ireland were dead-

BUSINESS SUMMARY

Granada set for £150m rights issue

Granada, UK leisure and television group, is expected to announce today a £150m rights issue and the departure of its chief executive Mr Derek Lewis.

The group's financial adviser, merchant bank S. G. Warburg, is believed to have been seeking the resignation of Mr Lewis as the price of going ahead with a rights issue to reduce the company's debt. Page 17

US EQUITIES rose sharply on futures-related buying. The Dow Jones Industrial Average reached its highest level since April 18, closing up 40.35 at 2,971.15. World stocks, Page 33

PROPERTY: The decline in commercial values should bottom out in the spring of 1992, according to prices posted in the first day of trading on the London Futures and Options Exchange's property futures market. Page 35; Fall in building output forecast, Page 3

JAPAN: Standard & Poor's, US rating agency, has placed the debt ratings of the four big Japanese securities houses under review for possible downgrading. Page 21

ALBANIA will introduce foreign investment, joint-venture legislation and measures to privatise sectors of the economy as part of a move to boost foreign trade and modernise

worst political crisis since the Second World War.

The eleventh-hour emergency mise – made against the backdrop of army threats to demobilisation of all citizens and police reservists in Croatia. It seems unlikely, however, given the deep distrust between Yugoslavia's two biggest ethnic groups, that either Serbs or Croats will comply with the order to hand over their weapons.

A statement from the president of Croatia, said it was "absolutely out of the question that Croatia's police reservists

YUGOSLAVIA yesterday inched back from the brink of civil war and military rule when the eight-member federal presidency agreed to give the army sweeping powers to end ethnic clashes in the republic of Croatia.

In a desperate effort to reach consensus after months of bitter disagreement, the collective presidency also agreed to form a commission to investigate the roots of the crisis. This is the first time the presidency has publicly acknowledged the ethnic nature of Yugoslavia's

authorities, prohibits the movement of any armed civilian units in unstable regions of the republic, and insists on the demobilisation of all citizens and police reservists in Croatia.

Mr Franjo Tudjman, president of Croatia, said it was "absolutely out of the question that Croatia's police reservists

would demobilise." In Belgrade, the federal capital and capital of the Republic of Serbia, thousands of demonstrators at what was originally a peace rally finished by calling for the establishment of a Serbian army.

The presidential agreement gives the army and federal police control over the predominantly Serbian territory of Krajina, in eastern Croatia. Krajina comprises about a third of Croatia's territory. But in a concession to Croatia, the statement recognised the inviolability of its borders, as sought by Croatian leaders.

Serbian leaders in Krajina have since August refused to allow Croatian police into the region, claiming that the police resemble the "Ustashe", the Nazi-backed Croat government set up during the Second World War.

Concern about the fate of Serbs in an independent Croatia has been manipulated by Serbia's communist authorities in order to gain support for their dispute with Croatia's pro-independence leaders.

The commission being set up under the agreement will include "legitimate" representatives from Croatia and the republic's Serbian minority.

However, its composition has already been criticised by Mr Tudjman. He said negotiations with Serbs could only include "the legitimately elected representatives to the Croatia parliament . . . [this] absolutely excludes Serbian leaders in rebel-held Knin [in the Krajina] who came to power through violence and terror".

Major to meet BMA on health reforms

By Alan Pike, Social Affairs Correspondent

THE prime minister yesterday agreed to meet leaders of Britain's doctors as the government faced political uproar over the effects of its health reforms.

Last month Mr John Major refused to meet British Medical Association leaders and rejected their claims that the National Health Service needed more money. The announcement that he will now see the doctors came as Mr William Waldegrave, the health secretary, failed to calm the BMA's general practitioners will receive preferential treatment

Dr Jeremy Lee-Potter, chairman of the BMA council, left a meeting with Mr Waldegrave yesterday saying he was "not

The NHS reforms – introduced only five weeks ago – have already confronted the government with three potentially damaging controversies.

Two of the new self-governing hospital trusts have announced up to 1,000 job losses because of financial problems; the Universities Funding Council and Committee of Vice-Chancellors and Principals has expressed fears that the reforms may damage medical education; and concern is mounting that patients of some general practitioners will receive preferential treatment in a two-tier hospital system.

Mr Waldegrave last night told the Royal College of General Practitioners the govern-

Alexander Bessmertnykh (left), Soviet foreign minister, is accompanied by his Syrian counterpart Farouq al-Sharah as he departs from Damascus airport after talks on a Middle East peace settlement. Page 16

OFT seeks power to probe cartels

The 'halo' effect of a publication on the brands or advertisements featured in its pages is thought to be greater where a publication has a clearly defined image, is seen to have a strong relationship with its readers, and where the brands or advertisements are relevant to the publication environment.

The *Financial Times* offers the best illustration of this point. It has a more clearly defined image than any other daily newspaper, and its readers are known to regard it as the authoritative source in the financial world. Hence the oft-spoken words, 'we must be in the *Financial Times*, because it provides authority and credibility within the senior business and financial community.' (How many times has that appeared in a media rationale?)

The extent to which a publication imposes its image on brands as opposed to the brand 'borrowing' from the medium is not clear.

> 'Publications do not necessarily impose their own image on the brands that they carry. A brand can borrow and feed off the brand values of a publication but it is a subtle and selective appropriation. Where the brand advertised has a clear empathy with a publication this "borrowing" probably takes place to a positive degree. However, where the brand/advertisement has a less clear relationship, then an association may not exist.'
> (*Alec Kenny, Managing Partner, Kenny, Lockett, Booth*)

Publishers, in particular women's magazine publishers, have long been advocates of the importance of media effect. It is seen as providing them with a competitive advantage over other media, beyond straightforward head counting. In his book, *A Complete Guide to Advertising*, Torin Douglas writes:

> 'The major advantage of most magazines is their editorial environment and authority which stems from the fact that they are reaching a specialist audience.... Research shows that many women like to see their weekly or monthly magazine as a friend, and that they regard advertising in magazines as more believable, helpful and appealing than on television.'

Without doubt, brands are placed in publications such as *Harpers & Queen*, *Vogue* and *World of Interiors* for image reasons as much as audience reasons. 'AS SEEN IN VOGUE' is headlined on showcards throughout the fashion retail trade. It's there because it makes a statement about the product or garment featured. It is 'borrowing' from the medium.

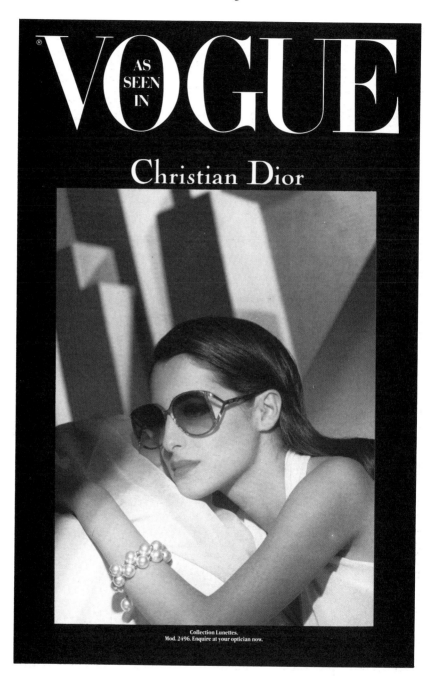

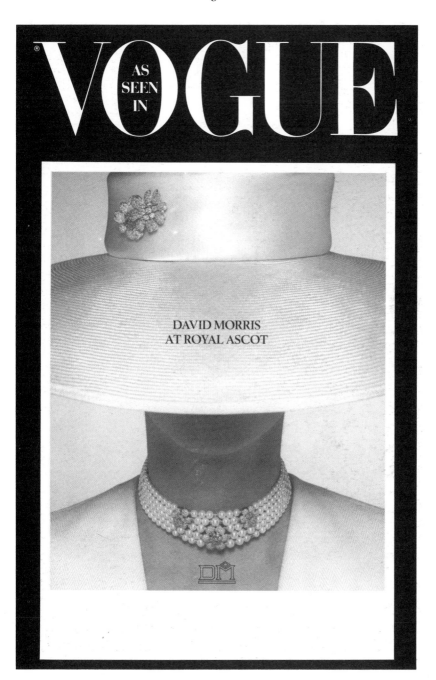

By the same token, brands appearing in publications such as *The Face*, *Q Magazine* and *Arena* can benefit from the clear imagery of those publications. But, to maximise that 'benefit', it makes sense that the brand and its treatment must have relevance and credibility, in respect of the publication in which it appears and the audience that the publication delivers.

THERE IS ONLY ONE DESERT BOOT

Clarks

THE ORIGINAL

[99]

The Clarks Desert Boot campaign unashamedly set out to 'borrow' from the image of the 'style' press. Clarks, a 'family' shoe manufacturer, had within its range a potentially high-fashion line – the desert boot. The advertisements were shot by Helmut Newton and placed in the 'style' press (*The Face, Arena,* etc). The company had on its hands a hugely successful campaign. Successful in terms of both sales and, importantly, in terms of the company's image. This is a perfect example of the benefits of a genuine fit between the product, the creative execution and the medium.

Complimentarity or Contrast

The press medium, unlike almost any other medium, is a collection of brands. It's clear, from both the buying and selling standpoints, that advertisements in the press medium are seen to work best when they are 'borrowing' from those brands' values. However, where 'complimentarity' is the order of the day, perhaps 'contrast' might provide a route to visibility.

Effective communication, however, has to do with much more than just standing out. Doubtless, a classicly brash supermarket price advertisement would stand out like a sore thumb in *Harpers & Queen*. And it's even possible that some of *Harpers & Queen*'s readers are interested in cut prices. (Maybe that's how some of them got rich in the first place!) But are they really interested when they are indulging themselves in the gloss and glamour of *Harpers & Queen?* Surely not. Equally, and just as importantly, should *Harpers & Queen* want to carry such ads?

Where advertising accounts for such a large proportion of a magazine's content, it must impact on the image of the magazine – its brand image. And that brand image has to be protected – even at the expense of advertising revenue.

Stephen Quinn, erstwhile publisher of *Harpers & Queen* and guardian of its elitist brand image once said: 'You will never see a Tesco advertisement in *Harpers & Queen*'.

He was probably right at the time. But times change, and even supermarkets, led largely by Sainsburys, are now responsible for some very elegant and tasteful price advertising – even *Harpers & Queen* couldn't resist it.

From Sainsbury's: the champagne they used to drink out of slippers. (Just slip us £6·45.)

It looks wonderfully wicked doesn't it?

Pink champagne has a glamour that few other drinks can match.

Yet no wine is more difficult to make.

It requires a long hot summer so that the mature red grapes can be picked late.

It needs expert timing. The skins of the grapes must be left in the juice for just so long (usually between 3 and 4 days) or what should be rosé turns out red.

The process is as painstaking as for all champagne but rather more unpredictable.

Which explains why you pay a little more for pink champagne and why so few houses produce it.

Our own pink champagne comes from the town of Epernay in the heart of the champagne district.

Some thirty-seven champagne firms have Epernay addresses and one of the streets in the town is called the 'Avenue de Champagne.'

Sainsbury's supplier is a small family concern that produces rosé brut champagne of exceptional quality.

The colour is delicate, the bubbles animated, the taste refreshingly dry and crisp.

It's difficult to ask more of any champagne. Particularly when we ask just £6.45 of you.

Good wine costs less at Sainsbury's.

Sainsbury's pink champagne as it appeared in Harper's & Queen

This short discussion of some of the accepted wisdom of media effect (an exhaustive discussion would probably fill up a whole book) indicates that it plays a significant part in the media-selection process. Much of this wisdom is based on hunch and inherited opinion. Investigative research seems to have played but a small part in the formulation of some of these widely-held and deep-seated views.

So, can research actually help in answering three important questions:

- Is there really such a thing as 'media effect'?
- Does it have an influence on brand image or advertisement communication?
- If it exists, in what way does it manifest itself?

While compiling this chapter, I commissioned a small qualitative study and uncovered a number of studies (carried out, largely, by or on behalf of publishers) into media effect. The main conclusions are set out below.

BRAND PERCEPTIONS IN THE CONTEXT OF A HOST MEDIUM: ANNETTE MATHERS (ABBOTT MEAD VICKERS/ SMS LIMITED — 1989)

In order to attempt to throw some light on consumer attitudes to brands in the context of the medium in which they appear, we undertook a small qualitative project. This consisted of four group discussions among BC1 adults aged 25–40, two male, two female.

During the course of each session, respondents were shown a number of magazines and newspapers. They were invited to talk about any advertising that attracted their attention against the background context of a discussion of their favourite publications and when and in what mood they read them.

THE USE OF COLOUR IN *THE TIMES* AND THE *TELEGRAPH*

Marks & Spencer in THE TIMES

Without any prompting, respondents in each group singled out a full-page colour execution for Marks & Spencer men's and women's clothing that was featured in the context of mainly black-and-white ads and features.

The same ad was also present in the *Independent* colour supplement, also looked at by each group, but in this context, it received no spontaneous mention.

In *The Times* there was a dual impact achieved both from the use of colour *per se* and the selection of that publication.

Respondents were impressed by the fact that Marks & Spencer was featured in such a large and expensive-looking advertisement, and in the newspaper that they associated with 'top people'.

The message that respondents took out about Marks & Spencer is clearly over and above that conveyed by the creative message:

> 'They must have spent a lot of money on it.'
> 'It puts them up with Simpsons and Austin Reed.'

So in this case the image attributes of *The Times* and the assumed cost of a full-page colour insertion conferred impressive values upon Marks & Spencer.

That respondents were enthusiastic is a mark of the high esteem in which they already held Marks & Spencer. There were indications that they would have been 'upset' to have seen a Marks & Spencer advertisement in the tabloid press, in that the quality perceptions of the Marks & Spencer brand would have been incongruous with the popular image of tabloids.

Tesco in the Telegraph

The use of two successive colour pages to feature Tesco Christmas grocery promotions was similarly full of impact. But in contrast to the Marks & Spencer execution, the attributes of the *Telegraph* were not automatically conferred upon Tesco.

In fact, perceptions of the appearance of Tesco advertising in the *Telegraph* were divided. Respondents were either very impressed or very cynical. In the former case, association with the values of the *Telegraph* was impressive because respondents were already aware that Tesco was improving its image:

> 'Tesco have changed their image over the last few years dramatically from cheapskate to quality.'

In other words, presence in the *Telegraph* was plausible and appropriate, and evidence of another step up the image scale.

But the alternative picture was based on the perceived incongruity of Tesco and the *Telegraph*. Those respondents who did not rate

Tesco highly were very *unimpressed* by the use of the *Telegraph*, which all regarded as an established, quality newspaper. The feature of grocery price promotions served to exacerbate the perception of incongruity:

'You're talking to the wrong people here.'
'It looks silly in this newspaper – mince pie prices.'

So for some respondents, the use of a quality medium for a lower quality brand had a negative effect.

Both the examples of Marks & Spencer and Tesco using colour insertions in the quality press demonstrate the potential of colour in a typically black-and-white context. But they also suggest that the choice of medium only works to help to build brand values if the reader believes that the brand already has the potential credentials. Where these credentials are in doubt, the dissonance between brand image and medium image may well have not only a neutral, but possibly even a detrimental effect.

THE 'MOOD' OF THE READER

The approach to a publication – the 'relationship' that a reader has with it – appears to have some bearing on the extent to which the medium's attributes can transfer to the brands advertised in it.

Our research suggested that a loyal reader who savoured his or her magazine in a leisurely indulgent mood was likely to transfer positive aspects of the magazine's imagery to brands advertised in it. This was particularly true of some women's magazines.

Cosmopolitan

Among the women recruited, there happened to be a high incidence of regular readers of *Cosmopolitan*. These *Cosmopolitan* readers claimed to have taken the magazine for at least ten years, and continued to rate it very highly.

The mood in which they read their magazine was very much one of indulgence. Unlike a newspaper or a colour supplement, which they claimed to glance at or 'pick up and put down', *Cosmopolitan* readers, along with those of other glossy magazines, sought a relaxed and peaceful time of day for a relaxed and indulgent read:

'I've got to be on my own.'
'I read it in the bath.'

The products these *Cosmopolitan* readers in our sample expected to see advertised were perfumes, skin creams, health-care products and lingerie. They claimed they approached these in the same way that they approached the magazine as a whole. In other words, they were in the frame of mind to study and enjoy the advertising as much as the features. They supported this by their recall of specific advertising, such as 'White Linen' by Estée Lauder, and skin cream from Lancôme.

What was particularly interesting was their perception of slightly more atypical products advertised in the editions of *Cosmopolitan* before them in the group.

A full-page advertisement for Lyons decaffeinated tea-bags was not considered at odds with the image of *Cosmopolitan*, but instead seems to have benefited from it, in that respondents assumed that the tea-bags were both healthy and trendy, because they were featured in *Cosmopolitan*.

> 'That's why they're in *Cosmopolitan*, because it must be a really hip thing to be drinking.'

Even an advertisement for British Coal gained from the same imagery. There was an assumption that there must be a new and 'healthy' message which, on closer inspection, was found.

> 'It's a green ad – they're trying to make it trendy – that's why it's in *Cosmopolitan*.'

So there was evidence from our research that a magazine with a very strong and well-defined image, such as *Cosmopolitan*, can influence readers' perceptions of brands advertised within it.

A single followed by a double-page spread for Next in *Vogue* was not singled out spontaneously for discussion, but was shown to respondents for their comments. The response tended to be divided between those who were impressed by what Next must be doing, and those who were very cynical.

Either:

> 'I'd think this must be quite interesting and I'd go to Next and have a look.'
> 'Next is on your High Street whereas everything in *Vogue* is designer this and designer that.'

or:

> 'I'd have never associated Next with *Vogue* – they must be desperate now.'

The latter group had read something about Next's financial state in the papers, and they were very cynical about its aspirations to be 'up to *Vogue*'.

The former group accepted that Next had the credentials to be in the company of *Vogue*, and mentally upgraded Next as a consequence.

The reactions to Next advertised in *Vogue* very much mirror those of Tesco advertised in the *Daily Telegraph*. Both these brand names appear to have positive images which can be enhanced by the media in which they are advertised, but both also carry a different set of imagery to other people, which appears in conflict with the medium in which they are advertised and which may be amplified as a consequence.

Woman/Bella, etc

The research indicated that women have a very different approach to readership of these publications. They are perceived as less escapist than *Cosmopolitan* or *Options*, less indulgent and less demanding. Their readers enjoy the short pieces, the 'snippets', and the factual information.

They claimed they would expect to see advertising for food and household products, ie correspondingly less indulgent products, and they were unlikely to spend as much time on them. As such, not surprisingly, there was little detailed recall of specific executions.

Overall, the research findings therefore suggest that the choice of press media to reach women may well have a significant bearing on their attitudes towards the brands they see advertised.

The media effect found appears to be a function of several factors:

• the 'mood' of the reader in approaching the medium;
• the reader's relationship with the publication;
• the 'fit' between the brand and the medium.

TELEVISION COMMERCIALS

Airtime and Weight of Advertising

In the discussion of television advertising, the research revealed a considerable sophistication in viewers' perceptions of the use of the medium by advertisers.

Both men and women were aware that the cost of going on TV is enormous and that, therefore, means big business. As such any brand that is seen on television is understood to be sizeable and serious in its intent.

Added to this, most respondents demonstrated a fairly sophisticated grasp of the significance of different airtime. It was apparent that different advertising appeared during different times of the day and during different programmes, targeted to reach the viewers at that time.

It was perceived that brands advertised during children's programmes were not for adults, and not likely to be personally very interesting or impressive. On the other hand, a brand advertised in *News at Ten* or a major feature film was interpreted as a major player, rubbing shoulders with leading names such as British Airways and Nescafé, as well as leading financial and corporate institutions.

Beyond the use of airtime, respondents also associated long commercials with high expenditure and a major selling effort. They also interpreted spectacularly unusual commercials in terms of time-length and/or position as indicative of a brand that was 'trying hard'.

The reel of commercials shown to respondents demonstrated that being on television is not enough *per se* to enhance the brand image if the creative vehicle is judged to be of inferior quality to the norm.

Respondents' reactions to a particular hay fever treatment showed a growing sophistication which is double-edged. For an OTC product to be advertised on television was greeted with interest, but the commercial itself was judged to be of poor quality.

The general feeling was that the product was not that well-established and probably not from a very large company, because they had not done a very 'professional' job.

Exclusive vs. Mass Brands

The reel of commercials shown in the groups was assembled to test out the hypothesis that television advertising might have a negative as well as a positive effect on brands, in that, as a broadcast medium, it might have the power to diminish the exclusivity of a name by over-exposure.

Respondents were shown commercials for Lanson Champagne and several leading perfume brands and again, without prompting, were invited to discuss the impressions they received.

The Lanson commercial was considered by both men and women to be very appealing in its use of music, its storyline, and black-and-white production.

The overall assessment was that the commercial had 'class'. This was important because, unlike the hay fever product example, the creative execution met with respondents' expectations and aspirations for champagne.

As to whether respondents found the use of television appropriate, or not, for champagne, the majority view was that most champagne is not exclusive anyway:

> 'Champagne isn't like it used to be – we all drink it occasionally.'

The fact that Lanson was the brand using television suggested that Lanson 'are trying hard':

> 'They want me to feel Lanson is well-known. It gives you a name to ask for.'
> 'It means they're trying hard but *they've not yet arrived*.'

This is significant, because there was a feeling that the most exclusive names do not advertise. As such, Moet et Chandon and Bollinger would not use television:

> 'They don't need to.'
> 'They're seen as expensive.'
> 'They have arrived.'

So in the case of Lanson Champagne, the use of the medium of television communicated that the brand was:

- affordable
- on the way up; *not* at the top.

The creative content helped to confer an image of class on the brand, but the use of TV *per se* meant to respondents that this was not an exclusive brand.

By the same token, television advertising for perfumes implied to the women we interviewed that the brands were big names, taking part in the big promotions, but the brands were affordable.

In the same way that they enjoyed perfume ads in their favourite magazines, respondents enjoyed a number of the commercials, especially for Beautiful, Ysatis, and Chanel. These were seen as tasteful advertisements with class and, again, the creative content was fundamental to the perception of the perfume image. Being on TV in itself did not diminish perceptions of these quality perfumes, because the creative execution was seen to be entirely appropriate.

But in line with champagne, it was felt that these were not *the* most exclusive perfumes. Really exclusive perfumes such as Joy and Giorgio did not use TV:

'They don't need to advertise on TV.'
'You never see Joy – it's very expensive and they like to stay exclusive – TV ads would make it a bit less exclusive.'

CONSUMER INTERPRETATION

An interesting overall impression that emerged from this study, and one which is increasingly evident, is that consumers are becoming more and more advertising-aware and, specifically, more media-aware. Media usage is being interpreted by consumers.

Despite the elegant and stylish Lanson execution it was still not considered an exclusive brand – *because it was on television*. How much of a risk was that; indeed, was it seen as a risk at all?

The answer lies in the balance between the advertiser's desire for exclusivity and his quest for volume. Lanson probably got the balance about right. The medium would have been instrumental in generating volume demand, but the power of the execution protected, indeed developed, the brand's classy, romantic image.

The Radion campaign, although not included in this study, provides an interesting, albeit very different angle on media effect. It is a campaign about visibility, about impact, about generating trial. It is a campaign that climbs above most others because, in its own way, be it on television or posters, it shouts loud.

It is not about the warmth, softness and family values associated with brands like Persil and Comfort. It is a no-nonsense approach. It is about getting rid of dirt and smells. 'It works, try it and see' is the sentiment.

Shout loud enough and often enough and people will hear. Radion is doing just that – functional advertising about a functional brand. The 'image' of the medium in which it appears is of little consequence. What is of consequence is that it is supported in major 'public' media (television and posters) and it is clear (even to consumers) that a huge amount of money is being invested in the campaign.

Media effect in this instance is not about image, but about size and scale.

PROJECT FUGITIVE: MARCH 1988

Project Fugitive, a qualitative study sponsored by the *Financial Times*, was a piece of experimental research designed to examine the differences in the messages picked up from colour advertisements in quality daily newspapers, and from the same advertisements in quality Sunday colour supplements.

The question that the research addressed was: 'What, if anything, does the medium itself contribute to readers' perceptions of specific colour advertisements?'

Among the conclusions drawn were the following:

- Quality daily newspapers can provide a context, a frame, which can give advertisements authority, news value and status.
- Being in colour in a quality daily newspaper greatly increases salience and the perceived status of the brand/advertiser, as well as clearly offering the opportunity to stand out from the editorial.
- Colour supplements give advertisements 'content value' only. They do not provide a 'frame' for special emphasis/elevation, but they do provide a gallery for exposure.
- To some extent, to optimise from the benefits of colour advertising in a quality daily newspaper, the advertisement should be integrated in tone, content or layout with other aspects of the newspaper.
- In a colour supplement, however, the colour advertisement must, above all, stand out from other advertisements and editorial in order to be successful.

THE PRESENTER EFFECT

A number of studies into 'the presenter effect' were carried out in the early 1970s by Alan Smith of IPC Magazines. He concluded that:

- Clear evidence is emerging that there is an interaction between the image of a media vehicle and associated advertising, and that this interaction can be measured.
- The effect will operate largely on the interpretation of the advertisement rather than on the image of the product itself, although there is, of course, no clear-cut dividing line between the two. However, *for well-established products* it seems fairly certain that the presenter effect is unlikely to have a discernible impact on the image of beliefs about the product itself, but it clearly may affect the message which readers or viewers receive about the product. On the other hand, *for new or unknown products* there is the possibility that the presenter effect may be far more powerful, and may produce shifts in perceived product attributes.

When summarising his work in this area, Alan Smith wrote:

'I am prepared to accept that the presenter effect exists and that more and more we will demonstrate significant shifts in communication performance. But what are these shifts worth? We are still faced with the problem of integrating results of the type I have demonstrated into cost per thousand OTS selection procedure and this, it seems to me, will always rely largely on judgement.'

BARCELONA READERSHIP RESEARCH SYMPOSIUM 1988

At the fourth international symposium held in Barcelona in 1988, Valentine Appel, senior vice-president and research director of Backer Spielvogel Bates Inc addressed the subject 'The Editorial Environment Controversy'.

In his opening remarks, Mr Appel said:

'Many magazine publishers and media buyers share the conviction that certain publications, by virtue of their unique editorial environments will either enhance or detract from the way in which advertising appearing in the publication will be perceived. For example, a 35mm camera when advertised in the pages of *Popular Photography* will be more favourably perceived than if the same ad were placed in a more general interest magazine such as *People* or *Reader's Digest*. An expensive wristwatch will be more favourably perceived if advertised in the pages of *Smithsonian* than in the pages of *Sport* or *Family Circle*. A liquor brand will be more favourably perceived if advertised in the pages of *Gourmet* rather than in the pages of *True Story* or the *National Enquirer*, etc.

The belief is widespread in the media buying community, despite the fact that no one has yet been able to design and execute a study to put the editorial environment hypothesis to a rigorous test: is it true that the same ad appearing in different magazines will be viewed differently depending upon the differences in their editorial environments?

This failure has not been for lack of trying. In addition to many unpublished studies – unpublished because they have unsuccessfully attempted to demonstrate the superiority of a given title *vis-à-vis* its competition – I am aware of nine studies that have been published in the US. All nine studies attempted to test the editorial environment hypothesis using samples of respondents who have been exposed to the same advertising in different publications and attempted to demonstrate that the respondents' perceptions of the ad had somehow been affected by the publication in which it appeared. Beginning with a study by *Fortune* in 1959, the most recent being one by *People* in 1986, none of these studies gives strong support to the editorial environment hypothesis, *regardless of the conclusions they may have reached*. Without exception, each of these studies either failed to find statistically significant differences between publications or was sufficiently flawed as to make the results of the study uninterpretable.'

What is interesting, however, and not altogether surprising, is that when looked at individually, the published reports of the studies (published, that is, by the commissioning media owners) do, in fact, draw very positive conclusions related to environmental or media effect/rub off.

The same is true of a recent study (1989) commissioned jointly by the National Magazine Company Ltd and Gruner & Jahr of the UK.

Women and Magazines – The Medium and the Message

The main conclusions of this study, in terms of media effect, were:

- Consumers expect the character, style and personality of an advertisement to be relevant to and compatible with the magazine.
- Further, they attribute some of the values of the magazine to the advertisements on its pages.
- Advertisements which conform most closely to the personality of the magazine will be most successful, as such advertisements reinforce the expectations and motivations which attract the reader to a particular magazine.
- A reader reads a magazine to take on the magazine personality's opinion – the closer the advertisements are to the magazine in character, the more authority they achieve.
- Because the personality of the supplement is ill-defined, advertisements do not gain endorsement from the supplement – any endorsement tends to come from the parent paper, which is regarded very much as the 'male' authority.

- 'Female' products when advertised in supplements are viewed negatively as very ordinary, down market and sometimes untrustworthy. Such advertisements also lack the authority given by women's magazines.
- Advertisements in women's magazines that are relevant to the character of the magazine carry the endorsement of its personality and achieve synergy with the content: this is enhanced if the advertisement is close to relevant editorial.
- The result is a 'dual branding' of the advertisement, a reinforcement coming from the magazine's own identity as a brand.
- In general, attributes of relevance, quality and trustworthiness are associated with women's magazines compared to supplements, and this is illustrated by the different perceptions of specific advertisements appearing in both media.

Doubtless, the findings of this study, because of its source, nature and structure, would sit alongside the nine US studies examined by Valentine Appel and be treated with similar caution – indeed, it is true to say that some of the conclusions are a reflection of interpretation rather than directly attributable to the evidence in the report. However, that is both a strength and a weakness of qualitative research.

The sample for this study was drawn substantially from regular readers of specified women's magazines, and it is not surprising, therefore, that they shared a strong relationship with their magazines:

'The reader/magazine relationship is special because the magazine reinforces the reader's identity as a particular kind of woman. Consequently, the reader/magazine relationship is very *personal* and affiliation with the magazine as a brand is very powerful.'

This relationship between a medium and its audience is a very significant factor in the media effect debate.

It seems clear that, on the one hand, the stronger the relationship between a publication and its reader, the greater the reader identification with the publication and the more likely it is that there will be a carry-over of media effect.

However, on the other hand, since different publications share different relationships with their readers and, at the same time, attract different levels of regular loyal readers, the nature and effect of the relationships becomes almost impossible to measure.

Studies carried out in Germany, sponsored by *Das Beste*, have, in conclusion, argued strongly that it is the strength of the reader/ magazine relationship that is the key factor in influencing media/ advertising effectiveness:

> 'The advertising value of a magazine is conclusively determined by the number of its readers with a close reader/magazine relationship.'

Not surprisingly, the studies show that *Das Beste*, with its high subscription level and loyalty of readership, scores well on the key criteria, and the report concludes 'It pays to advertise in *Das Beste*'. Nothing too subtle about that!

The Medium – Viewer/Reader Relationship

The consumption of media can be identified on two levels. First, on a physical level, ie the when and where of media consumption, and second, on a further emotional level, ie the frame of mind of the reader/viewer/listener when consuming the media.

If, as I believe, the media/user relationship is at the heart of media effect, it is no surprise that it has proved difficult, if not impossible, to measure.

What is required, and what is now being undertaken by many agencies, is continuous qualitative research that probes the depths of the media/user relationship in order to provide a richer understanding of the role of media in people's lives on both an emotional as well as a rational level. Why is it important to try to understand the nature of that relationship? It is so because the indications are that the strength and nature of that relationship can have a direct bearing on the level of media effect.

Regularity and loyalty of readership are available measures that are indicative of the strength of a publication/reader relationship. Indeed many of the conclusions drawn in the publisher – commissioned studies into media effect are questioned on the basis of sample bias towards regular readers. That in itself says something about the relationship between media effect and regular readers.

SUMMARY AND CONCLUSIONS

It is too easy to dismiss the phenomenon of media effect on the grounds that there is insufficient conclusive evidence to support its existence. However, leading academics and researchers have, in fact, taken this position. In open discussion at the 1988 Barcelona Readership Symposium, no less an authority than Harry Henry was reported as follows:

> 'Harry Henry (UK) said that Val Appel had shown how it had proved impossible in the past to identify or measure rub-off effect and had explained the difficulty the Advertising Research Foundation was having in trying to do either. In his experience, both as Managing Director of a major research company and as Marketing Director of a large publishing house, he had spent a great deal of time on that particular problem – in the one case making a lot of money, and in the other spending a lot of money. He had been left with the conviction that *the effect did not exist*. Obviously, if it did not exist it was not difficult to understand why it could not be either identified or measured: one might as well try to capture a will-o'-the-wisp and put it in a box. Perhaps the attempt should be given up.'

I believe, however, that the medium does contribute to both advertising effect and brand perception. Our inability to measure the phenomenon does not provide sufficient reason to deny its existence.

Certainly, none of the many (in excess of 20) studies and papers on the subject produced over the last 30 years have, individually, provided definitive conclusions or hard data acceptable to the research purist. However, they have, in my opinion, provided in total, many clues, indications and suggestions which, coupled with anecdotal evidence lead to both reasonable and useful conclusions.

1. There appear to be two kinds of media effect, namely 'total' effect and 'immediate environment' effect, ie the influence of the medium itself and the influence of the environment within a given medium. Both types of media effect can have an impact upon brand perceptions and advertising effectiveness. The medium itself would appear to have a more significant impact on brand perceptions, while the immediate environment would appear to have a more significant impact on advertising effectiveness.

2. The extent of media effect appears to depend upon three things, namely:
    a) the relationship between the viewer/reader/listener and the medium;
    b) the image of the medium as a brand;
    c) the relevance of the brand/advertising message to the medium and its audience.

3. The clearer the image of a medium as a brand, the greater the likelihood that there will be a transfer of that image to the brands that it carries.

4. A brand that is relevant to the medium within which it appears is more likely to benefit from the image of that medium.

5. Media effect is subordinate to the creative communication. Thus, a relatively upmarket, image-based product will not suffer, in perception terms, from appearing in a mass medium, such as television, provided the creative treatment is executed in a manner consistent with the brand's image.

Brand perceptions are developed over time. And brand perceptions may well be attributable, in part, to a long-term association with a medium. Because of changes and evolution within the media, across the population and within brands themselves, the significance of this association will never be proven. I have no doubt, however, that it exists.

Nothing undertaken in the last 35 years detracts from John Hobson's view that 'media effect will always be largely a matter of common sense and informed perception.'

CHAPTER FIVE

Competitive Marketing

STEPHEN J WOODWARD

Stephen Woodward was appointed chief executive officer to Ayer in November 1990 and assumed full management control and day-to-day responsibility for the Agency's activities in the UK.

He was formerly CEO of the brands division of Michael Peters, management group head of Lowe Howard-Spink, and marketing director of Seagram UK. At Michael Peters he was responsible for their UK brands companies which merged to form the brands division. At Lowe Howard-Spink his group was responsible for the award-winning Whitbread Ales campaign, Heineken, Stella Artois, British Rail corporate and Imperial Tobacco accounts. At Seagram, he launched Paul Masson and was responsible for brands such as Chivas Regal, Mumm Champagne, Captain Morgan and Sandeman.

CHAPTER FIVE

Competitive Marketing

STEPHEN WOODWARD

The best business education that I ever received did not come from my lecturers at business school, nor from a 'guru' on a marketing conference platform, or any of the managers for whom I have worked. It came from an uncle who, for a long time, was responsible for the UK's external telecommunications, putting up satellites such as the Intelsat that made this country a world leader in that field.

As is often the case, the advice came in the form of a dressing-down. I was asked as a marketing man what books were in my library. I proudly reeled off list after list of titles from Drucher to Kotler, and while I did so his eyes gradually closed – it was a reflection of my own myopia.

The dressing-down commenced: 'Yes', he said, 'but what else?' Indignantly, I explained that there were a large number of books on marketing and strategy; how was I expected to read them all? 'I agree', he said, 'but what else?' I enthused about Edward de Bono, and by this stage was perplexed to say the least, but still I did not convince him. After what seemed like an interminable pause, he proceeded to complete my business education.

Why did I not have any books on war, the great battles and the great generals? Why did I not have any books on sport, the great captains and managers? Why did I not have any books on chess, the great games, the great masters? The reason why I should, he explained, is very simple: business, and particularly marketing, is competitive. It is a war, a sport, an intellectual challenge, all rolled into one. The rules and lessons of each apply and are equally relevant. The fundamentals require a plan of campaign which has both a short-term and a long-term perspective. The plan must define the goal, or set of goals; the strategy, or means by which the goals are to be achieved – including contingencies for all possible actions and reactions; and the tactics which will need to be employed.

This advice has been invaluable, both as a source of good reading as well as excellent business education.

THE GAME PLAN AND YOUR OPPONENT

Whether fighting a war, taking part in an important match, or competing against another company or brand, if you want to win, it is vital that you know the plan, or likely plan, of your opponent. Only under these circumstances will you really be able to judge whether it is worth competing in the first place; whether you have the ability to win; and the method most likely to provide the best chance of success.

Most marketeers focus on the consumer, yet competitive success requires not only complete knowledge of the consumer and his needs and motivations, but also complete knowledge of the opponent: his goals; all the forces at his disposal; the game plans that he has used in the past, (both successfully and unsuccessfully) and is likely to use in the future; and his psychology, both as a team and individually. It demands that you have the same objective knowledge of your opponents as you do of your own position – in all respects.

If one reads about Nelson at Trafalgar, Wellington at Waterloo, Montgomery at Alamein, the 49ers at the 24th Superbowl, Alan Bond in the 1984 Americas Cup, or Korchnoy against Karpov, the opponent has always been a key focus. The leaders and the winners throughout history know as much and sometimes more about their opponents than their opponents do. Ask any general or top sports manager about his opponents in a major game or championship – he will talk about their complete record, their resources and players, their strategies and tactics, where, how and when they fight or play best. He will know the effect of any weakness, how it will change their strategies and their tactics.

If you do not hold this kind of information about your competitors, you do not deserve to win. Even if you do manage to win a number of skirmishes or battles in the short term, you will certainly have less chance of winning in the long term.

COMPANY COMMITMENT

It is no coincidence that the vocabulary of modern sport today is very similar to the vocabulary of war; that as much time is spent analysing the opponent, his people and hardware, his strategy and tactics, as is spent devising and practising one's own game plan. That practice, drill, and discipline is key to making the team play as a totality – not as a collection of individuals – with awareness of the goals and the means by which to achieve them shared by all players.

However, the same is still not yet true of many of today's marketing companies. In its strangely jargonistic professional-speak, it is fashionable to talk about marketing as a culture, not a department – though it is still too often merely a department. It is fashionable to talk about the necessity for good internal communications, but most people in a company still don't know the goals of the organisation or the means by which it is planned to achieve them. It is fashionable to talk of teamwork, but in fact many company members do not feel that they are part of any team.

The major marketing companies tend to win because they achieve these things better than others. For IBM, Mars, Procter and Gamble, Nestlé, and Unilever, the sense of belonging inherent in their culture is as important to their success as their sheer size and momentum. Their drill, discipline, belief in what and how they do things enables this to happen. Equally, smaller companies that have achieved much success in a short period of time have done so through their culture as much as with their brands. Apple Computers, Phileas Fogg and Body Shop are all examples of jointly-shared and focused commitment.

This culture should coincide with another dimension that the marketing world all too often pretends to believe and practice, but which is rarely rigorously achieved – this is the true nature of being market-driven.

Marketing and branding is about recognising customer or consumer needs, harnessing them, and satisfying them in a competitive and constantly-changing marketplace. The days of being a producer of products, rather than a marketeer of branded goods and services, are over. Companies fail every day because they are still either fundamentally or culturally producers of products, rather than completely committed marketeers of brands. They do not adjust their brands or strategies over time; many move backwards from being marketeers of brands to producers of products; many brands and companies have failed because their market has progressed, while they have not. True brand marketeers recognise that consumer needs change over time.

The Corporate Brand

It is not insignificant that the growth in the so-called corporate identity business has been due to the recognition by corporate officers that their entire company is a brand. By treating it as such they can achieve a shared commitment to building that brand, so that their audience, be it the City, shareholders, employees, clients or customers, can better understand what the brand is and what it stands for. Companies who work with major consultancies to redefine their corporate identity or corporate branding, often do so in a more rigorous, complete and holistic manner than the professional marketeer who is involved in product branding.

We are now at a time when there is a growing recognition that brands are in reality loaned to a company by its consumers. A corporate brand is owned by the various types of consumer of corporate brands. Those consumers may be the shareholders, the City, employees or customers. If the corporate brand is not well positioned, if it does not have a clear proposition, or does not deliver that proposition, it is less likely to appeal than a competitive brand. A product brand works in exactly the same way. If it does not satisfy its market need with a clear positioning, and the proposition that it delivers, it will fail against the competitor that does.

It is something of an indictment that the concept that has brought the notion of brands to the forefront has been brand valuation, and that it has been the accountant, not the marketeer, who developed this concept. Perhaps the reason for this is that the marketeer often remains tied to the product, and has failed to communicate what the brand is all about. There are, after all, still a large number of companies who use the term 'product management', not 'brand management' – a symptom of the problem.

BRAND POSITIONING

The critical point of this understanding is to be able to communicate a brand's positioning, and proposition. Marketeers must recognise that for this to be effectively achieved with the consumer, it must first be achieved within their company and their chain of supply. Any poorly positioned brand without a valid proposition is likely to be undermined by a stronger competitor, or positioned alternatively by one of the many channels of distribution. A typical manifestation of this is when supermarkets cut a brand's price, or its range. In effect, they have repositioned the brand, and very often the brand owner has let them do so without complaint, without thinking beyond the 'price' effect to the 'brand' effect.

Understanding of brands within marketing departments, and beyond them into the whole company, can be achieved through exercises and group discussion. Given that any brand is a mix of image and substance, the best starting-point is often an exercise in understanding brand positioning related to substance: what the product is and does in isolation and in relation to its competitors. This can be described as product interrogation. Understanding its image can then be introduced through exercises such as brand personality interrogation. If the brand were a person, who would it be? These types of exercises allow real understanding of a brand to be achieved and communicated. This understanding is as critical for the competitor brands as it is for your own.

Brand Personality

Ultimately the consumer has to build a relationship with a brand for it to have any strength or staying-power. This is why 'brand personality' has developed as a term. Humans react in human ways. Relationships develop through awareness and familiarity and then people decide from this whether they want to know more about a person, become friends, and the strength of that friendship. Relationships with brands develop in the same manner. If, therefore, a brand's positioning is not clear – if its personality is not clear – then consumers are likely, through lack of understanding or of trust, to reject the brand for one that they do understand.

The much-used term 'synergy', or consistency of message, is therefore critical to the communication of a brand. If messages are confused, if the brand personality is out of focus or split, then the brand has the potential to be rejected by consumers and undermined by competition.

Part of the understanding of this is also associated with a real understanding of the role that the brand plays in the lives of its consumers. In the same way that people have friends or acquaintances who fit into different parts of their lives, this is true of brands. The role may be functional – the new Radion detergent has a focused, strong product appeal, and a focused helpful personality – or the role may be principally image – Chivas Regal is actually positioned against brands such as Hermes scarves and Gucci, around the world – it says more about you than American Express ever can.

Any communication through advertising, PR, sponsorship, design, product development, pricing, or where and how a brand is stocked and merchandised can add to or detract from the positioning. Even corporate brands such as Shell can suffer markedly if its message, 'environmentally responsible' is spoilt through accident or design. A focused, clear personality, linked with the right positioning will achieve immense power, but always remember that it will also be more at risk of confusion – if you know someone well and they do something out of character, you will notice it more than if you did not know them well.

The personality is, in effect, the essence of the corporate or product brand. It is as important for it to have values that it represents – for which it stands – as it is to have product-based characteristics. This is what the marketing world means by adding value. The term should really be 'adding values'. An understanding of the values that will result in positive consumer response, and an understanding of how to modify or create them in order to achieve a focused brand personality, are the critical requirements of the marketeer.

Brand Extension

It is this practice that is forming the basis of the new methodologies in brand extension. Given the above, a brand can 'own' a certain territory, but good brand extension can also use the values appropriately to extend that territory. For example, Volvo cars are seen as responsible protectors, but not as performance cars. The launch of their new sports car had to have a visual image of sportiness, but carry the fundamental qualities of the Volvo design look, and therefore continue to communicate protection. As long as it showed a picture of the car and logo, the advertising communication would primarily talk of performance; protection would be taken as read. If, however, the design had not had a Volvo family look, then the car might have been a problem – it may have undermined the parent brand's values.

If a brand's identity and its product performance are therefore in *continuous* communication with the consumer, this communication can be developed in order to develop the brand. It must not contradict. It can surprise, but it must not contradict.

A brand extension gives to, and takes from the parent brand; any brand may need to adjust its personality over time to remain relevant. It does not do this in isolation, but in the context of its competitors and the entire market-place. How to achieve this comes back to the basics of good marketing practice, and the analogy of fighting a war, or winning at sport: the rigour of achieving complete

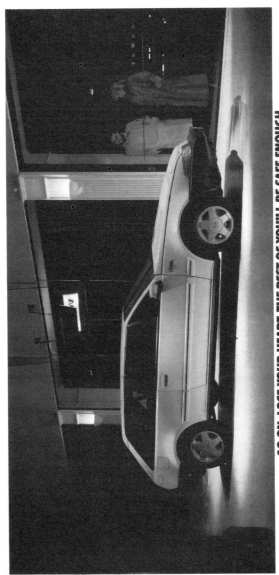

knowledge, and defining how the goals are to be achieved. This is soundly acknowledged at the advertising agency, J Walter Thomson, who always ask five fundamental questions:

- Where are we now?
- Why are we there?
- Where could we be?
- How do we get there?
- Are we getting there?

These fundamental questions have been asked by all the world's great generals, leaders, and sport managers. The answers require absolute knowledge and information, the understanding of what that knowledge actually means or could mean, and the inspiration and vision to translate that knowledge into achievable goals.

From this they can establish a plan for achievement, and objectively assess whether the goals are being achieved or whether they need to be reassessed. Whether one is marketing a corporate or a product brand, those responsible for its management should be asking these fundamental questions continuously, to enable them to achieve the best possible positioning for their brand, with such a focus that they attain and remain in the strongest, most competitive market position.

Critical to this knowledge is an understanding of the process of consumption in any particular market. The customer or consumer of any goods or services acts in a series of basic ways. He or she has a need, and whether it is conscious or subconscious, it is an actual or potential need, that will change over time through the function of time.

Maslow's hierarchy of needs should be helpful to any marketeer as part of needs definition and understanding. Look at how far it goes to explaining how the current environmental awareness has allowed companies to market products such as unleaded petrol, which even five years ago would not have been considered worthwhile, while other products, such as non-CFC aerosols, can die just as quickly. Maslow would argue that society moves to the next level when it has achieved material satisfaction, and that material considerations then include the air, the earth and the atmosphere. Those who have recognised this have achieved a lot, but those who have not risk major losses of market share, profitability, or an entire brand.

Maslow's five levels of needs

Competitive Brand Assessment

Competitive brand assessment is very often insufficiently thorough. It demands rigour and tends to use hard data. It should measure product range, pricing, availability, market share, and rates of sale through all distribution channels. It should also consider product quality and performance, customer service, and analysis of historic patterns of all marketing support, from media strategy to promotions and PR.

Too often competitive assessment is based on cursory one-time measures for SWOT analysis, or Boston grids. If tracking a competitor's patterns of behaviour does not take place over time, then much of the analysis is worthless. Equally, simple screening of elements such as media spot-buying strategy can achieve enormous increases in understanding of competitor behaviour and of market response dynamics.

At the same time, an understanding of the competitive brands' soft values are vital, yet rarely achieved. So called 'brand valuation' has tended to rely on hard data, and can be a useful aid to judging a competitor's brand strength, but there is a significant difference between brand value and brand values.

Soft values include a brand's positioning and proposition in terms of brand personality, image, and the territory it may own or aspire to owning. Regular use of qualitative clinics are crucial to this knowledge, and this means going beyond group discussions to measuring individual components of branding, such as the advertising or packaging. It means assessing all the elements that create or influence the image and the actuality of the brand – together.

During the 1980s, brands such as Captain Morgan Rum used such techniques to clearly identify their core brand values and how they were differentiated from their competitors – such as Lambs. Captain Morgan established the clear positioning of 'Genuine Caribbean Rum' versus Lambs' '1940s and the Cruel Sea'. By focusing all advertising, PR and promotion on this theme, Captain Morgan distanced itself from Lambs, both in positioning and brand share. It allowed a clear brand proposition – and no more sponsorship of fishing tournaments, or tailor-made promotions to win a weekend for two in Paris that had been allowed to happen in the past. It also established normative soft data which not only informed all aspects of the marketing mix, but enabled the tracking of brand values over time, to ensure that the brand retained relevance, and to check whether there were market movements against it.

Whitbread in the UK have achieved the same with Stella Artois lager by identifying a positioning based on premium product quality, in a market obsessed with image values. Product quality positioning defined a territory for Stella Artois that informs all of the marketing mix, and can be regularly tracked to ensure that the territory remains relevant and is understood. True synergy has been achieved where no element of branding is allowed to be at odds with the positioning.

Through this type of understanding, marketeers can ensure that the brand is clearly differentiated from the competition and remains clearly focused in the mind's eye of the consumer. *This can only be achieved by conducting the exercise on a continuous basis, and by doing it for all competing brands as rigorously as one does for one's own.*

Competitor Assessment

In the same way that one needs to know one's own corporate goals, the structure for managing them, and the individuals who work in the organisation, so one needs to know this information about competitors. What is the importance of any brand to the competitor? How high is it on the priority list for investment or support? How important a profit-contributor is it? Who is managing the brand, the marketing team, the sales force? Have you ever met them? Do you know people who know them? What is their track record? How well, or quickly do they react? Which agencies, and what type of agencies do they use? What are their patterns of behaviour? Knowing the answers to these questions will enable you to determine what kind of action or reaction you will get to any strategy or tactic you adopt.

Clearly, different companies have a culture or style that affects the way they manage their business and brands. When Seagram launched the brand Crocodillo in direct competition to Allied-Lyons Babycham, competitive analysis enabled many potential pitfalls to be avoided, but was not sufficient to judge the most significant: it was well-known that the Showering's family wealth and domination of Allied-Lyons came from the success of Babycham. The family's emotional commitment to the brand was enormous, and as a result when attacked by Crocodillo, one of the family members on the main board of Allied-Lyons took control as brand manager of Babycham. The investment made by Allied-Lyons in defence of Babycham was enormous, and much greater than the brand warranted in business terms.

How many competitors will fight this hard, are prepared, or even able to spend well over the odds in defence of their brands? This kind of understanding is fundamental to achieving success.

If you know that a competitor may have a supply problem with materials or finished product, if you know he has a quality problem, or that his sales team is now headed by a manager who favours discounting, you can be in an extremely strong competitive position. Changes of agency invariably mean a change of strategy – one ought to know what the options could be.

When it was leaked that CDP were to handle the launch of a new Lever Bros detergent, 'Breeze', Proctor and Gamble should have been able to judge the likely brand positioning and proposition. CDP rarely run USP-type advertising, so Breeze was bound to be positioned on an emotional proposition, in a different segment to other Lever brands.

Changes of ownership can dramatically change business strategy – one ought to know the options or likely outcomes. When Hanson bought the Imperial Group, Gallaher should have been able to judge the likely change of Imperial strategy. Hanson requires a tough return on asset performance, that would demand brand rationalisation to achieve a leaner portfolio, with significant delisting of low volume, weak brands.

Economic or political change may affect a market, or a brand – again, one ought to know the options or likely outcomes. With East and West Germany now united, many of the companies that were split East–West in the post-war period must be considering reunifying themselves. Which are those companies? What could the effect be? The Schott glass company was split post-war, with separate companies in East and West Germany. If it reunifies, it will become a major force both in Eastern and in Western Europe. The potential effect on other major European glass companies would be enormous.

It is a battle, it is a sport – sometimes the plan may be for attack, often it may be for defence, and there will be nothing more important than arming oneself with an absolute understanding of the opponent and the battlefield.

MARKETING TOOLS VERSUS BUSINESS TOOLS

Business and marketing plans should be devised and assessed not only for one's own company or brand, but also for the competitors, taking account of all the available elements – not only the hardware in the armoury, but also the software. Too often, marketeers think narrowly of only marketing tools, when all the available corporate business tools should be assessed and interrogated, if necessary using internal research or brainstorming, to judge how they may help to achieve competitive success.

The *corporate resource* may allow reciprocal deals or joint ventures with other companies in your supply chain, with overseas companies, even with other companies within your own group. Shared investment or funding, shared information, or shared cost utilisation may present real opportunities. The transfer of knowledge from one industry to another could be used more in technical problem-solving.

Efficiency, sometimes but not always linked with cost-cutting, can often provide the source of funding required for brand-building; it can achieve improvements of quality, or it can reduce reaction or lead times. *Financial resources* are often not interrogated sufficiently as part of the planning process. Can equipment be leased or rented, rather than purchased? Can advertising production costs be spread over the life cycle of an advertisement, rather than written off immediately? Can the sales force be supplemented with a freelance or part-time resource in order to reduce overhead costs, and to free-up funding for brand-building? Again, competitor information can help in this area.

When the Monopolies Commission released their report on the petfood industry in the mid-1970s, much of the information it provided about the capital and materials funding of Pedigree Petfoods was of immense help in guiding the future capital and work-in-progress funding of their competitors.

The *human resource* is another increasingly important area of competitive advantage for any company. It was Avis who harnessed this in such a powerful way, with the development of their 'We try harder' campaign. The whole of the company was drawn together with a strategy that communicated a clear proposition to customers, delivered by the staff.

Similarly the British Airways proposition, 'The world's favourite airline', was devised as a valid claim which could be made to customers (BA carried more passengers than any other airline) – but one with which those customers had to agree if it was to have credibility. BA set about this by a complete culture change within the company. Staff training and commitment to customer care was achieved, so that customers began rating it as their favourite choice to fly – and then the advertising claim was launched.

It is apparent that, as with the use of marketing tools, these broader business tools cannot be successfully brought into play without clear and complete communication. It is important to ask in real terms how often members of a company, its supply chain, and its customer chain, know what the goals and plans actually are? How often do they know who the competitors really are? How often do they know who their leaders or brand champions are?

Communication is crucial to knowing what people are supposed to be doing, and what is expected of them. It is no good telling them about the new advertising campaign if they don't know what their *own* role is, let alone the role of the advertising. In all too many cases, people do not feel part of the team, or do not know who the other members of the team are. If they do not know what each component does then, unwittingly or not, they may work against what the others are trying to achieve.

The corporate culture is crucial. So-called market or marketing-driven companies still have much less of a consumer or customer-led culture than their marketing services advisors. Advertising, design, and promotional agencies will live and breathe the consumer; the brand owner rarely achieves this position. Yet if one is to be successful, one has to achieve the reality of such a culture, and it is no good the marketing man and his agency taking this view if the rest of the company do not share or understand it.

The corporate or product brand has to be continuously scrutinised, and when necessary strategy or tactics must be changed. Its competitors and its market also have to be continuously scrutinised. Its owners and staff, their goals and their strategies, must too come under constant scrutiny. As changes occur during a war, or a football match, so the general, the manager or the player, has to decide to continue with the game plan or to adjust. The same applies with the brand.

To recall my uncle – playing chess against him had some similarities to competitive marketing – he used to tell me that if at some stage in a game I felt I'd rather have his colour, I probably knew I was getting it wrong and was going to lose.

If you would rather be on your opponent's side, marketing his company or brand, you probably know already that you've got it wrong.

The problem is, you could be just as likely to get his brand wrong as well. To have a better chance, think of your competitors as real opponents, compete with them totally, and you are likely to have a greater chance of winning.

Brand Packaging

MARY LEWIS

Mary Lewis is creative director of Lewis Moberly. She graduated from Camberwell School of Art, and then studied as a postgraduate at the Central School of Art. Her career began as a fine art printmaker and lecturer in graphic design. In 1984 she founded Lewis Moberly with partner Robert Moberly. The company has won numerous awards, including the British Design & Art Direction Gold Award for Outstanding Design, two Silver Awards for Packaging, and twenty Clio Gold Awards for International Packaging Design. Its work has been profiled and exhibited extensively in Europe, America, Japan and the USSR. Mary has been a recent member of the Design and Art Direction Executive Committee and is a fellow of the Royal Society of Arts.

CHAPTER SIX

Brand Packaging

MARY LEWIS

Back in the days when ranchers branded their cattle – one of the earliest and most rudimentary forms of brand packaging – the message was 'hands off'. Now the message to consumers from branded goods is 'hands on', and the more the better. But there are ways and ways of having a dialogue with the consumer through the message and impact of the pack: more and more marketeers are discovering that there is a commercial advantage to be gained if the pack does more than simply remind people that 'I'm here'. Ideally it should project a personality, instil loyalty, forge emotional links, and actively persuade people to 'buy me'.

Packaging design has become 'active'. An exciting new agenda has been set which combines the creative with the commercial, and explores the intuitive alongside the rational. Packaging design has emerged from obscurity to become a potent marketing vehicle and a rewarding advertising medium. Factors behind the development of active packaging, and the lessons for all those involved in building profitable brands, form the substance of this chapter.

The issues of good brand packaging go right to the heart of commercial performance, because the pack is the physical embodiment of a brand's core values. The pack evokes the essence of what the brand is all about. It is the brand's identity.

Brands, like people, have personalities. But unlike people, brands are consistent and reliable. They 'never' let you down (Perrier was a rare, swiftly rectified slip). Yet it is the unpredictability of people which makes them interesting and gives them their charm. Does this mean we should design unpredictability into brands? I return to this later in the chapter.

Just as people 'brand' themselves through their personal packaging to signify a sense of personality, or identify with a particular group, so brands can be designed to communicate certain cultural values to enable the consumer to 'belong'. The brand becomes an extension of ourselves. We are what we buy.

Therefore the most fundamental aspect of good brand packaging relates to establishing character or personality, building the elements which make the brand recognisable, visible and individual – packaging which says 'Trust me, buy me, I am for you'.

A dialogue with the consumer via the pack is potent marketing. 'Talking' packs intrigue, inform, involve, entertain and persuade. They engage the consumer at the point of sale for a few valuable moments – time to make a sale. They can beckon you down the aisle, or stop you dead in your tracks. Either way they have your attention.

But good brand packaging is far more than a salesman. It is also a flag of recognition and a symbol of values. To understand this complex role let's first define the brand. The product is the physical property that is purchased. The brand is the aura of beliefs and expectations about the product which make it relevant and distinctive. It stretches beyond the physical into the psychological, and is extremely powerful.

Expectation of 'performance' is one of the most important dimensions of a brand, and could be described as the arbiter of the amount you are willing to pay over and above the cost of the raw materials inside the pack.

A pile of white powder by itself is just that: you certainly would not have the confidence to sprinkle it over your new baby. Put the powder inside a pack called Johnson's, and emotions are immediately evoked of the caring nature of the mother–child relationship. You would certainly trust the product with your baby. You would not be willing to pay much, if anything, for the powder alone. You would be willing to pay a premium for a brand you trust and believe in.

Clearly, differentiation of this kind is all in the mind. The white powder does not change at all. Yet the expression of brand values makes all the difference. Brands, therefore, only really exist in the minds of people, and could be said to belong to the consumer rather than the manufacturer. Commercial events have proved this point: when Coca-Cola was forced by consumer pressure to withdraw 'new' Coke and bring back the original, Coca-Cola's European Community president, Ralph Cooper said it was evidence that the brand belonged to the people, and not to the company.

One of the key roles of brand packaging is to assist in the process of selection of goods. Ten years ago the typical supermarket was a 'noisy' place, as brands tried to outshout each other. Wall-to-wall logos screamed for attention, aggressive colours flashed out signals. Manufacturers established their brand values primarily through TV and poster advertising, and used their packs merely as a visual 'trigger' for the advertising message.

But while this route reminded consumers of the brand story, it did not extend or enhance the story. It moved the branded message on from the 'hands off' of the cattle rancher to the hands-on 'recognise me' of the modern marketeer. Today's 'active' packaging fulfils a more important role as a medium in its own right. It is still capable of delivering a singular message as part of the brand story, but it is also capable of more subtle, sophisticated interpretation. It does not just say 'here I am': it says 'try me, I'm for you'.

Analysis of what makes brand packaging active is best approached via examples of what, in my view, is working on the supermarket shelves today. It is only by comparison of various branded goods that the important factors which contribute to successful packaging design can be highlighted.

IN SEARCH OF GOOD PACKAGING DESIGN

What gives good brand packaging its edge? The objectives are many. It must flag down the prospect in mass display; involve on an emotional level, strike a chord, touch a nerve; symbolise the brand's core proposition and differentiate it from the competition; project the brand's personality; persuade and seduce; communicate information; provide a functional cover for the product in transit and in the home; and be ecologically friendly. A tall order.

Brand packaging continues to work after purchase: for example, at home; in the bathroom; in the kitchen; and on the table – often for weeks on end. We were brought up with the friendly faces of Kelloggs, Heinz, Cadbury's, and Johnson's Baby. They are part of life. But where it works hardest is at the point of sale, at the critical moment when the purchase decision is made. It is scarcely possible to overestimate the power of packaging to influence brand choice.

Focusing on the supermarket, where most brand choices are made, it is easy to identify three broad types of decision: those which are taken on 'automatic pilot', usually staple products to replace larder stock; the experimental purchase, where the pack either suggests an idea or links to one already in the mind at low saliency put there perhaps by editorial, an ad or personal recommendation; and finally the indulgent, spontaneous purchase. But you cannot force products or brands into these categories. For example, pizza used to be an experimental product, now it's a staple for many families. A Mars bar can be a lorry driver's staple or a secretary's indulgence.

With these potential pitfalls of classification in clear view, it is possible to examine different brand packaging in action.

TRIGGER PACKS

It goes without saying that the most famous brands have stood the test of time because they have continued to meet a consumer need and have sustained a competitive advantage. But two other factors have often been involved. They have been built on the power of advertising, and they are the product of the vision of one person or a small group. Ford, MacDonalds, Mars, Cadbury, Kelloggs, Coca-Cola, Rolls-Royce, the list is endless. The differentiating philosophy of these companies was laid down in the early years, long before the power and role of design was fully recognised or understood.

The prime requirement from packaging was recognition – hence the dominance of wall-to-wall logos, often in the form of the founder's signature (genuine or contrived), like Cadbury and Kelloggs.

The trigger pack is the extreme case of putting recognition before everything else. Heinz Baked Beans is an example: it simply says 'I'm here' and, in contrast to more active packaging, there is no added value other than pure recognition. Its design elements do nothing other than adopt a strong, confident voice to trigger the associations built up by the brand's advertising and experience of the product over the years. Oxo and Nivea are further examples.

More recent developments in brand packaging suggest that trigger packs can miss a trick. Trigger packs do work – but they are vulnerable. At a time when design in general is playing a broader aspirational role, trigger packs are too often impersonal and devoid of emotion. They shout loud but say little.

One step forward is the logo plus time-honoured symbol. These packs operate largely on the trigger principle, but don't have the arrogance to assume that logo alone will suffice. Fairy Liquid (Baby), Dettol (Sword), Colmans Mustard (Bull's Head) all make strong visual statements with clarity and dignity. They add values to the pack through symbols which then become properties or equities of the brand. 'Look no further', they say, and with effect.

The toothpaste market gives another example, but using graphics instead of symbols. Colgate and Macleans show the logo in a classic trigger situation. SR, by contrast, evokes whiteness and brightness through the analogy of mountain and snow, a long-term brand property. It isn't a question of one being right and the other wrong, because packaging is only one means of talking to the consumer. What is certain, however, is that on its own the SR pack works a lot harder and says a great deal more.

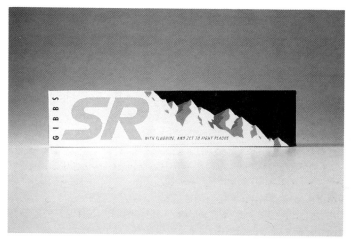

Trigger plus

CORPORATE VERSUS PRODUCT BRANDING

There are classically two opposite approaches to branding. There is the corporate approach, where all the products of a company are branded with the company name – an extreme case being Yamaha, covering everything from organs to motor bikes to yachts. In packaged goods Heinz is another good example.

The opposite approach makes each individual product a brand in its own right, ignoring or disowning its parentage. The category in which this used to be the governing philosophy is detergents – Persil, Daz, Omo, etc, but interestingly in recent years Lever Brothers have added a Lever endorsement, in order to get the best of both worlds. Another classic example is Mars, who sell Mars, Snickers, Bounty etc as unconnected brands, other than the address in small print on the back. But here again, only last year a failing product, Applause, was given an overt Mars endorsement to boost its flagging fortunes.

In between these two extremes lie a range of different levels of overt corporate endorsement. The car market is a typical example from Ford Fiesta to Ferrari Testarossa. In packaged goods we have Kellogg's Corn Flakes – clearly a brand, yet 'Corn Flakes' is but an unregisterable product description.

Cadbury's Dairy Milk chocolate bar and Cadbury's Milk Tray are two separate brands talking to different audiences. CDM is a self purchase with sharing potential. Milk Tray is an easy gift for low profile occasions. They share strong traditional Cadbury's chocolate values, and hence the dominance of Cadbury purple is appropriate. Other products within the Cadbury stable, eg Smash and Marvel had little coherence with the core values, and it was not therefore surprising that they could be floated off into a separate company with a separate identity, ultimately losing their Cadbury endorsement altogether.

Which brand structure is best suited depends partly on the corporate culture of the company. From a market and consumer viewpoint it depends on the extent to which shared values and authority are credible and motivating to the consumer. I would not salivate over a box of Boeing chocolates, nor would I take off happily in a Cadbury aircraft.

I believe Marks & Spencer sandwiches taste better and have more imaginative fillings than my local sandwich shop, but I really doubt the effectiveness of their washing-up liquid, particularly when it is dressed in the piped music, pretty pastels world they have adopted as corporate styling for everything from shampoos to detergents.

Consumers are intelligent about brands. They understand the game and are willing players. They can distinguish between the brand values of a product and the brand values of a company. Even with a single product brand, it is possible in research to tease out the image of the company separately from the image of the brand.

This is where packaging design plays a major role. It has the ability to communicate through words and images very precise expectations, attitudes and positioning. We can detect movement on a range of image scales from point (a) to point (b) according to fairly minor changes in visual emphasis. The start point for good brand packaging is a clear understanding of where we are now and where we want to be.

THE CORPORATE BLANKET

The trend in the eighties has been to stretch brands to cover a wider set of products. As brand owners have discovered the power of what they own, it has been easier and far cheaper to stretch a brand than to create a new one. But there are dangers in the corporate blanket approach.

Kellogg's (whether Corn Flakes or All-Bran) demonstrates the format look, with all the elements in their predetermined place on a closely-monitored grid. It works – but only to a point, because such a design strait-jacket inhibits the 'active' development of sub-brands aimed at different targets. Small brands, however, are often forced to adopt this approach, at the expense of their individual offering. For them the corporate blanket is a means of saying 'I exist' over and over again.

Retailers used to take this approach, notably the now defunct Fine Fare, who created an inflexible design grid across all categories. Soup looked like tights looked like cereals. The blanket was too all-embracing. The packs could not fight within their category.

If the core values associated with the brand can be applied to other markets, then the established brand identity can often take the brand into those markets. Lucozade is an example of successful brand-stretch through packaging. The original design has been accented to pick up the flavour of new, albeit closely-related, markets – Sport, Light etc. A more radical brand extension, that of the confectionery brand Mars into the ice-cream sector has also made use of the same key visual equities – the brand name, logostyle and colours.

Corporate branding to a fault

NEW BRANDS

When inviting people to experiment with a new brand, more chances must be taken, and the risks are greater. Phileas Fogg, I believe, succeeded. Its involving, distinctive packaging immediately sets up a dialogue with the consumer by expressing the idea that 'if the story's worth telling, it's an interesting product'. At the time of its launch, the Phileas Fogg graphic approach was highly unusual: a unique point of difference was established via design creativity, making the packs enticing, intriguing and importantly collectable.

Phileas Fogg has proven itself in performance to be an excellent example of active packaging. So has Winalot Prime from Spillers. In a bid to gain a foothold in a market dominated by the Mars brand Pedigree Chum, the design concept was created to forge an emotional bond with owners of dogs and to reflect an innovative product. Each flavour variant features a different dog in a country setting – an aspirational note for all urban dog owners. In addition the design approach broke the mould of a classic trigger pack category, dominated by wall-to-wall logos, obligatory dog's head and elementary colour coding.

By tapping into what it feels like to own and care for a dog, through sensitive and involving graphics, this example of active packaging enabled Spillers to successfully enter a tough market. But for every success story, new brands waste the chance for active packaging. Take Sheba, for example: this was an innovative product story and packaging form in a traditionally conservative 'me too' category. But it missed a golden opportunity...instead of gourmet cat food, could it be cat litter? Cat-on-the-mat graphics are unsubtle, and suggest a mass market commodity. Successful it may be, but is it as successful as it could be?

NURTURING FAMOUS BRANDS

Aside from the tricky business of persuading the consumer to try totally new brands, famous, long-established brands are part of our cultural heritage – reassuring landmarks with familiar friendly faces. Sometimes the guardians of these brands lose confidence in them, betray their sense of vision and allow brand character to be diminished. However, some of the best packaging design in recent memory has been in the skilful updating of successful brands, 'moving on' the brand without the consumer even noticing.

Anchor Butter, Dettol, Fairy Liquid, Persil and Lea & Perrins are all good examples of this. Anchor Butter is a household name, a confident brand leader. Our brief was to retain its status, capitalise on its strength and exploit its command of multi-facings in-store. Importantly, the housewife was to have no sense of a new design – she can quickly link change of pack to change of product.

The new design makes the leader's logo the hero, adds movement, which increases in-store impact, and clears the pack of unnecessary clutter. She knows how much it weighs, therefore relegate this information to the back of the pack and give the important elements space.

Skilful update

An outstanding example of a brand confidently retaining its cultural tradition is Marmite. So strong is its visual branding that it can put a simple 'My Mate' on a hoarding as a form of shorthand, and the consumer gets the message. Surprising, therefore, that Bovril, from the same stable, should throw its heritage away. Less surprising are the sales results. Bovril, the one-time leader, is struggling. Marmite has forged ahead.

Updating famous brands is a highly specialised and sensitive skill. Unfortunately the exercise too often suffers from 'a little knowledge' on the part of the brand's guardians. Valuable equities often go unrecognized, and feelings wrongly run high on irrelevant visual details. Many brand packs lose the opportunity to be more coherent in their message, because the equities have been wrongly assessed.

Confidently retaining its cultural tradition

[145]

The pack designer plays an important role in this assessment. A trained eye can strip the pack to its bare essentials and then carefully build on its strength. Prejudice, affection and boredom must equally be as carefully considered. Too close to the brand, too fond of the brand or (probably worse) bored with the brand, are danger areas. Too often they lead to the wrong brief and reason for change.

RADICAL REPOSITIONING

In the delicate business of repositioning brands, the packaging is frequently more important than the advertising, because it forcefully defines the new frame through which you want the consumer to see the brand. In this context, active packaging gives the marketing process broader options.

Complan, for example, was historically positioned as a product for the sick and elderly before it was completely redesigned in order to talk to a new market of young people, closet Complan users. The old pack for the 'complete meal in a drink' resembled a get-well card, its graphics reminiscent of retirement home ads. The radical new look features bright, bold illustrations conveying an image of health, fun and fitness. A life-plan for Complan. The singular aim was to break down prejudice about the brand: to tell young people that, far from gruel for the toothless, Complan is a convenience product for people of all ages to eat 'anytime, any place, anywhere'.

Limmits packaging had become party to the cliché graphics of the category. White packs with wishy-washy images or tape measure graphics. In the growing meal-replacement market there was an opportunity for Limmits to lead and touch a new nerve, vanity. Consumers want reassurance of the end result, not the process or problem. New Limmits packaging plays up to this idea. Slim, black, 'sexy' packs appeal to the self-conscious. 'I want to look like those packs' said one respondent....

Radical repositioning is not for the faint-hearted. Brands have a natural life cycle. Products and images can be locked forever in time warps. Our nostalgic affection for them too often becomes an obstacle in the 'relevance to today' stakes. As lifestyles and behavioural patterns change, many brands will need reassessment, or be in danger of dying with their market. If the brand's heritage has been nurtured, the consumer's confidence can be transferred to the new positioning without loss of face, giving renewed energy to the life-force of the brand.

Get well card

Lifeplan for Complan

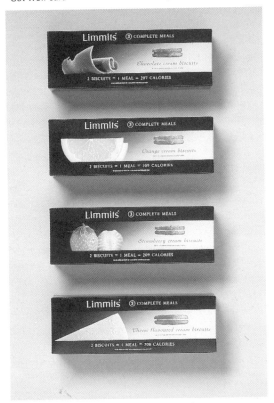

I want to look like those packs

Understanding Brands

VARIETY IS THE SPICE OF LIFE!

Danger: brands can become boring...

Earlier I touched on the parallel between brands and people, and the unpredictable qualities of the latter. Whereas the majority of brands stay in repetitive territory, some brands make variety a property. Penguin, the biscuit bar brand, is sold in multipacks of six, and each pack shows a penguin in a different pose, thus bringing alive the advertising proposition of 'pick up a Penguin [and have fun]'. The variety of executions of the penguin make him a larger character than a single figure could ever have hoped to do.

Phillip Morris launched a new brand of cigarette in Switzerland, a highly competitive market where over 200 brands jostle for kiosk space. Certain visual rules tend to apply to the packaging in the global cigarette market; red signifies strong tar, fading through the warm browns and yellows of the mid tar packs to the snowy white low tar offerings. Slim packs are for female smokers, and soft packs for the macho individualists.

The new brand broke all the rules. The only consistent aspects were the cigarette, the standard carton shape and the brand name Star. Every six months a new series of graphic imagery graced the packaging. There were no crests or bars of colour, but rather leopard spots, desert islands and Rennie Mackintosh grids. Soon the brand had achieved a significant share, with each new series of packaging designs eagerly awaited. The Swatch concept had been successfully transferred to the tobacco market.

Even more interesting considerations arise if, rather than the product remaining constant with the brand identity changing, the product changes with the brand identity remaining constant. Freshly-squeezed orange juice is now readily available from many large supermarkets, yet the product changes from day to day dependent on the raw oranges used. Indeed, it is because the product changes that you know it really *is* freshly squeezed. The packaging however, remains constant.

In a more controllable way, Rowntree teased their fans with mysterious, extraterrestrial blue smarties several years ago. The question was, would you find a blue smartie in a particular pack? This year, with Rowntree's new relationship with Nestlé, the hunt is on for the elusive white smartie. These minor product changes have been responsible for increased sales.

Cadbury's latest mega-launch is a brand called Strollers, a bag full of three separate chocolate-coated variants: caramel, raisins and biscuits. They all look the same, so you don't know what you are eating until it's in your mouth. A good way to build in surprise, but the packaging fails to embrace this point of difference. Is this a lost opportunity? I believe so.

The new Covent Garden Soup Company has a range of fresh soups sold in cartons. As the seasons change, a new soup is available on-shelf, which exploits the seasonal produce of that particular month. The essence of the brand, ie freshness, is reinforced by these introductions. The packaging remains constant, with an applied sticky label to communicate the new soup variety.

Some brands rely heavily on their consistency both in product and brand identity terms; a sudden change in baby food packaging could cause alarm rather than interest. However, on many brands, particularly those appealing to the young or young at heart, it can be worth re-examining the brief to see if changing the design of either the product or the packaging can create an additional dynamic.

The lesson is, as always, avoid a formulaic approach. Go to the root of the problem and apply creatively fresh thinking to the solution.

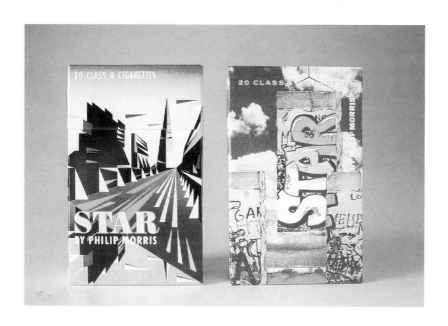

Every picture tells a story

CULT BRANDS

There is a type of branded pack which comes under the cult heading. Packs in this category defy time, stay resolutely true to their character and are totally believable. They may not epitomise 'good' design, but they are intangibly compelling. A favourite of mine is Angostura Bitters: its label is too big and the copy is too small, but there's a wealth of history here – a truly defiant individual. Contrast that with Café Crème, which was much loved as an 'undesigned' cult brand. Its appeal was that it looked like it had never been anywhere near a brand manager or pack designer. Yet its identity was carelessly thrown away with a squeaky clean redesign which balanced up all the elements to create blandness.

A truly defiant individual

Brand Packaging

Certain categories defy the marketeer or designer, and need to be tackled by experienced hands. In the drinks market authenticity plays a dominant role, and the designer's understanding of how authenticity is achieved is crucial.

Lagavulin, a malt whisky brand owned by United Distillers, betrayed designer indulgence to the point at which a redesign was necessary to tone down the fun and games and re-establish the heritage. The designer tricks much in evidence on the previous packaging were discarded in favour of a more restrained respect for tradition. Label, cork, cap and carton reaffirmed the brand's authenticity by capturing the essence of the historic distillery on Islay where the whisky is made and taking a trip back through the island's visual history. The skill of the packaging designer is probably never more critical than when subtle nuances and 'unmarketed' imagery form the integrity of the brand and the beliefs that surround it.

This is an instance when the results of good design have been measured. Lagavulin is one of six malts marketed under the Classic Malts banner – all of which have been redesigned, together with collateral material. With no other media involved, these are the results:

	1987	1988	1989	1990
Classic Malts *Ex Factory Volume Index*	100	104 ↑ Relaunch	291	689

In an attempt to be all things to all people, many brands lose their focus and many packs lose their impact. A good brand pack must be single-minded and able to eyeball with the consumer. The pack has a very short time-slot on shelf, and its message must be concise.

Three factors contribute to packaging overload. One is a lack of understanding of pace, ie how the consumer moves towards the pack through the store. Second is the brief which asks for far too much, ie too many messages to be delivered at one time, and third is the proliferation of information that the consumer has come to expect in respect of the product and its use.

A successful pack cannot be expected to deliver all. In the broader arena it interleaves with advertising and point of sale. In the local arena its format is restrictive and its backdrop visually busy. A carefully considered assessment of priorities is necessary to establish a logical order of communication. An understanding of how the consumer shops for a particular product is essential. Is she on automatic pilot or just cruising? The pack will need to respond very differently.

Complicated coding and conceptual mysteries abound on our supermarket shelves. Aspirational buys wear everyday clothes, and shopping-list items are too often overdressed.

The hosiery market is notoriously overloaded. Ask any woman if she enjoys buying what should be a pleasurable personal product, and she will invariably say no. Packaging is a visual porridge of anarchic coding and layered information.

Designers inspired by the fashion aspect of the brief create atmospheric concepts which in turn fight with crucial information regarding denier, size, style and colour. Boots have recently tackled this problem head-on with a totally new approach to their hosiery packaging. Clear, concise information is hero. The obligatory window depicting the product avoids being a bolt-on afterthought by becoming central to the idea, showing the product where the woman most wants to see it, on her legs.

Selection made easy

By restricting colour coding, clearly identifying the product and carefully pacing the information, selection is made easy, cohesion and impact is achieved on-shelf and the shopping experience can once more be pleasurable.

HOLISTIC SOLUTIONS

Some highly visible brands, however, need no graphic composition. The brand lives through its form. This is extremely active packaging, denoting a kind of shorthand between brand and consumer. The use of three-dimensional aspects of packaging to build brand loyalty is often overlooked. Now more than ever holistic packaging solutions in which pack form and function play a major role are on the increase.

The links between packaging design and product design are closer than is sometimes imagined. What, after all, does a product designer do when creating a new telephone but create packaging for the mechanical and electronic components?

A successful combination of both two-dimensional and three-dimensional pack elements can be highly profitable. L'eggs, the largest-selling brand of hosiery in the world, owes much of its success to its innovative and differentiating pack format, the famous egg-shaped container.

Jiff Lemon uses form in the most direct way possible. Here the form is the product. Rapport, a new product from Shulton in the mass male fragrance market, is another example of integrated form and graphics. Teamwork between advertising agency Tony Hodges & Partners, research consultancy David Young & Associates, design consultancy Lewis Moberly, and the client produced the most successful new product launch ever in the male fragrance market. Rapport moved quietly into a category dominated by noisy macho brands of the eighties. Appealing to the sensitive 90s man, confident of his masculinty, the new brand carved out a new category. Name, form and tactile experience combined to create a dialogue with the consumer.

Brand name Rapport underscores the new sensitivity. The unique rhomboid shape is subtle and intriguing. In turn the silky, acid etched finish is smooth and sensual. The form is echoed in the pack graphics. The story is extended to the advertising, where black-and-white monotone images provide the perfect backdrop to the warm red brand colour.

Again sales results are convincing. Rapport has not only succeeded in building a new 'volume prestige' market, it dominates with a 24 per cent market share. The auditing company quote it as 'the most successful new male fragrance launch ever'. This was partnership with advertising, but the packaging role was critical.

Many experienced marketeers now understand the importance of a singular vision in design. The new brand whose form, graphics and advertising are considered separately is in danger of bit-part playing.

'Intelligent' brands often show an alliance of this kind. Crown's Advance – a transparent, square paint box – is both intelligent and innovative. The DIY shelves groan with paint cans screaming colour. But which colour? The consumer only wants the one in the pack! Crown's see-through pack solves the problem in one. The pack form is the hero and the dominant brand equity. In contrast, brand leader Dulux's Kitchens and Bathroom paint compounds the problem: consumers must fight through an attention-grabbing barrage of colours and graphics to find the all-important paint reference. This is not only a lost opportunity for the brand, but a competitive opportunity for the own brand.

Asda's paints took up the challenge. Paint cans traditionally are printed in bulk and then sport an applied label to the front face of the cans to display the accurate colour reference. Without exception it sits unsympathetically on complex graphics which confuse the colour selection. Asda Paints turn this necessity into a virtue. The 'problem' sticky label becomes the hero, clearly focusing the all-important colour and becoming the star of the show.

Most successful new product launch

ADVERTISING IDEAS TRANSFERRED TO PACKAGING

Pack designers are in the business of building relationships, whether between the brand and consumers, the pack form and the surface graphics, or the pack message and the product advertising. Often packs are created which are dependent on advertising. As discussed earlier, there are trigger packs whose sole aim is to remind the consumer of the values created through advertising. But some packs go further, and take the advertising idea as the core packaging idea. There are dangers inherent in this approach.

Sometimes it can work: Sure deodorant uses the anti-perspirant tick symbol from the commercials as a recognisable device on the packs. This long-lasting advertising idea translates well to the more permanent, constant media of pack design.

But often it doesn't. Anchor Real Dairy Cream, for example has taken the popular dancing cows from the Saatchi TV commercial as the illustration for the pack. What will happen to the pack when the advertising campaign inevitably changes? Will the pack's image in turn dance around? The dancing cows concept is humorous, and funny ads are replaced more swiftly because the public tires of the joke. Packs for major brands need to be more enduring.

Need to be more enduring

Understanding Brands

PACKAGING IDEAS INTEGRAL TO ADVERTISING

If it is the role of brand packaging to actively project a brand's personality and quality, then surely the advertising campaign should emerge from the core values of the packaging. It is not impossible – albeit rare. Saatchi & Saatchi, the agency which created the Anchor Cream dancing cows, also developed advertising based on the core packaging idea we created for Johnson & Johnson's European brand Silhouettes.

The Silhouettes pack communicates the superior performance of this Sanpro brand by featuring an origami bird, state of the art in paper performance and suggestive of balance, precision and strength – the ultimate symbol of superior lightness and absorbency. The Saatchi advertisement for Silhouettes adopts the packaging idea. The origami bird literally flies on to the pack after it has been drinking from a pool to demonstrate its absorbent qualities. The brand values and loyalty established by the pack graphics are carried expertly over into the advertising, with the result that the overall marketing message has a strong synergy, important for a new brand which needs to establish itself with one cohesive message.

Too often, product advertising wastes or ignores the fundamental imagery or idea of the pack design. How often have you watched a brilliant 60-second TV commercial and then been unable to recall the name of the brand it was advertising? This failure of recognition could be overcome if pack and ad worked more closely together. As a packaging designer, I believe either discipline can take the lead role – there is, after all, no set formula in these things and examples have shown it can work well either way, so long as there is synergy in the creative approach.

The truth is that the stronger and more visually relevant the pack, the more the creative team in the advertising agency will want to feature it in the commercial. Silhouettes bears this out. If the pack is ugly and out of step with the brand values, then it will be relegated to a tiny packshot at the end of the spot. Battles follow between client and agency, with the packaging designer often a helpless onlooker. Active packaging, then, has broader benefits for marketeers. Its integrated presence as a dialogue-builder in advertising will help to prevent the chronic branding problems of those commercials which are forced against their will to end up on the 'packshot'.

State of art, paper performance

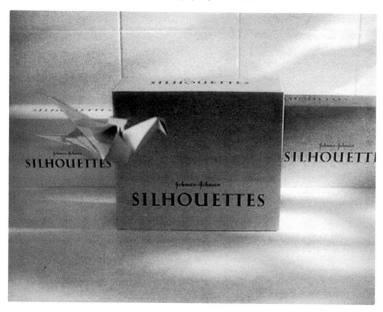

Strong synergy

A FREE ADVERTISING MEDIUM

The relationship between packaging and advertising in building profitable brands is today under unprecedented scrutiny, because it is now more widely recognised that packaging is actually a free advertising medium. It has taken a long time for this to gel in marketing circles – perhaps because things that are free are immediately undervalued.

For a long time opportunities went unexploited, because pack designers didn't realise the value of what they were selling and clients didn't realise the value of what they were buying. In selling design too cheaply, consultancies did a disservice to the significance of their solutions. Packaging design, though, is an extraordinarily effective piece of media buying in terms of cost and penetration. Whereas you pay for the media space in TV or press advertising, in packaging you own the space. The media space element is entirely free, projecting your message on supermarket shelves and in transit, and continuing to communicate brand values in the home.

There is no doubt that advertising is a powerful way to build ideas around a brand; its influence in short, sharp bursts has an intensity which helps to turn and direct the flywheel of the brand. Packaging performs the same brand-building function, but burns at a slower rate. It works for 52 weeks a year, is wrapped around the product at point of purchase (the perfect medium), and is the last and sometimes only chance to make a sale.

Yet this form of permanent medium has been entirely wasted by generations of marketeers, simply because it doesn't show up in the normal way on a conventional marketing budget. But if you assess its worth in terms of 'opportunity cost' on a brand manager's balance sheet, failure to get the pack design right is the equivalent of squandering millions in a normal media budget.

Then there are the brands for whom packaging is the only medium through which to communicate to the consumer; their owners cannot afford the big budgets to mount a TV campaign, so astute investment in design can make a smaller amount of money in the marketing budget go a very long way.

OWN LABEL, THE CATALYST

To those who say that the rise in the importance of packaging design has been sudden and dramatic in recent years, packaging designers are likely to reply: 'Why did it take so long?' Reasons for the brand packaging revolution, if that is what it has been, can be traced to the evolution of own-label goods in the UK over the past decade. The rise of retail power in the early 1980s concentrated economic leverage in the hands of a few multiple food chains. Retailers such as Marks & Spencer and Tesco began to set a standard in own-label products which in turn affected the way manufacturers designed their top-selling brands. The retailers were proactive, and many brands became reactive.

Historically the own-label product was a cheap and cheerful brand imitation for those who couldn't afford the real thing. It didn't have quite the quality, but then it wasn't quite the price. Tesco in particular pioneered a new understanding of the power of design. Aware that it could develop own-label merchandise to dominate the bottom end of the market, it began to upgrade quality and design in order to compete directly with manufacturer's brands. In parallel, the new own-label merchandise in the stores was of a similar quality to the brands, but was often better looking, cheaper in price and 'active' in enticing consumers. Meanwhile the latter had also moved ahead. A new, discerning and design-literate customer was entering the stores, educated and stimulated by the high street package deal design boom. Famous names suddenly looked vulnerable – the main strategic weapon in the retailers' offensive was good-looking packaging design.

It was an offensive confined to the UK. In America, the 'private label' movement did not take on board the message of innovative design in the same way. There, own-label design consisted of developing a pack as close to the brand as possible, without actually being taken to court. But in Britain, food stores began to establish formidable own-label brands – without recognisable brand names. Safeway's Shortbread range is an example of a strong creative concept making up for the lack of an immediate name to project. The imaginative stitched label becomes the brand name replacement.

As the standard of own-label packaging rose, so stores were able to establish their corporate personae through the goods on their shelves. Asda's wines and spirits range is an example of building identity via an own-label programme. Recognised as a breakthrough, the packaging debunked 'mass design for mass taste'. Sophisticated abstract images created 'art for the people' at a price they could afford. Asda's brave approach has increased sales year on year. Established brands, some of which had been resting on their laurels for decades, were now under threat. The fight-back was not long in coming.

Art for the people

BRANDS FIGHT BACK

Brand owners, believing that you fight fire with fire, looked to designers to revitalise their brands. But one of the major problems they faced in fighting back against the design-led encroachment of own-label was in knowing when and how to revise the packaging without putting a highly recognisable, time-honoured brand at risk.

This will be familiar to any brand manager setting a design brief, and any designer endeavouring to answer it: how do you attract a new audience without alienating the existing one?

The conflict between tradition and change often worries manufacturers a great deal more than consumers, who turn out to be a lot less protective of old values than is commonly imagined. Manufacturers often fret over what they regard to be a radical leap into the dark – and then the consumer doesn't even notice there has been a change.

There is an additional problem of well-liked brands creating a 'halo effect' over the brand packaging, which can mislead market research. This was evident in a major redesign programme carried out for Cadbury's Milk Tray. People questioned about the brand tended to defend the packaging because they loved the chocolates and loved the advertising, and regarded any critical question of the pack as an assault on the brand itself.

This loyalty to the pack can sometimes be misread. It is sometimes used as a rationale to leave unchanged packaging which patently needs to be updated and which consumers actually dislike. It is just that they inadvertently defend the packaging because they want to defend the brand. This happened initially in the case of Milk Tray, which Cadbury perceived as needing a redesign in order to increase its performance in the gift market. Once the halo effect was identified, however, research gave a truer reading as the project developed.

Designers should identify the true equities of the brand which must be retailed at all costs. The revision of famous brand identities is too often regarded as a stark choice between total revolution and subtle evolution, neither of which may truly satisfy market needs.

Identifying the valuable visual equity of a brand is as much an instinctive assessment as a rational one – it can be achieved using conventional research techniques in which a pack design is progressively stripped of its elements, or by the designer who visually abstracts the pack to establish its true picture. Retain the right elements and you are free to develop the relationship with the consumer.

Johnson & Johnson's Carefree is an example of maintaining a brand's familiarity, while moving it on significantly in terms of positioning. The logo and background colour were changed in an evolutionary way – a subtle enhancement. But an entirely new image was introduced: a handkerchief, actively symbolising that the product, a panty shield, was the finishing touch to a woman's everyday wardrobe, and not just a once-a-month necessity. The brand has advanced in the way it has disassociated itself from the unpleasantness of Sanpro and established itself as a daily hygiene product. However, it remains instantly recognisable to existing customers, because a clever graphic game has been played. The handkerchief idea on the new pack graphically mirrors the old product picture on the former pack. The same amount of colour distribution enables the pack to be both different and the same. It appears as an old friend but delivers a new message.

Brand revisions such as Carefree show that it needn't always be a case of evolution versus revolution. Active packaging can give the owner of the brand more options to retain the old audience while enticing the new.

Old friend delivers new message

EVALUATING PACK CHANGES

In the course of revising famous brands, manufacturers inevitably seek sensible ways to evaluate pack design changes among consumers. Pack designers too are seeking greater accountability, and look to research to give them a clearer understanding of their creative task. Often the challenge of separating packaging from other elements of the marketing mix can seem daunting, but only by trying will a body of knowledge accrue from which reasonable judgements can be made.

However, the entire question of pack evaluation by the public is problematic. Market research has been too often responsible for derailing innovative design ideas which, if given the chance, might have gone like a train in the market-place. The sophisticated, multi-faceted discipline of planning has a far greater future in the design industry. It handles the tools with sensitivity.

But in this area I have a simple rule. It is this: don't set up members of the public as aesthetic critics, don't ask them to judge the design of packs. Their opinions on typefaces or images are of little value, and dangerously misleading. Instead, gauge their emotional response to packs in an indirect way, for example by disguising packaging research under the guise of product research.

We recently presented five bottles to a consumer panel, each with a different label but identical contents. We asked their opinion of the product's taste. The bottle with the more elegant label was described as having a more refined taste; the bottle with the macho label was perceived as having a stronger flavour, and so on. Their responses told us much about the impact of the different graphics we had created, and reaffirmed how effectively images can affect taste, and how powerful is the potential of packaging design. We did not ask them a single question about the graphics. Effective pack research measures communication and emotional response. Bad pack research sets the consumer up as design critic.

But the most valuable use of research in developing brand packaging is before design takes place. Who are we talking to? What makes them tick? What are their visual points of reference? How do they shop for our brand? What responses does the existing pack evoke? What new responses are desired? Which visual elements are equities to be retained? Which are category language, and therefore useful positioning support? Which are irrelevant or downright misleading?

There is great scope for planners, researchers and designers to develop a better understanding of how design works, and new techniques for arriving at these answers. We are developing a dedicated planning model which is not 'on loan' from advertising. Design is multi-sensual and works in different ways through time and space. The advertising analogy can be useful, but is far from the whole truth.

At the end of the day we must convince clients that design is highly cost effective. It is a mark of new maturity within the design profession that the Design Business Association (equivalent of the IPA) was formed in 1986, leading to the first Design Effectiveness Award Scheme in 1989.

Ironically the scheme has got off to a slow start through lack of client interest. It's hard enough to prove the effectiveness of design against all other elements of the mix without having your hands tied behind your back. But soon the penny (or is it a million?) will drop, and well-managed creative design will be recognised for its full worth.

Packaging design has been a much-neglected partner in the business of building brands. A whole new chapter is now being written.

The underlying message is this. The pack embodies the brand. It has the power to engage the consumer in dialogue at the very moment the purchase decision is made. It can work for the brand or against it. It can make or break a sale. There is no formula for doing it well. It requires talent, understanding, sensitivity and experience. It is a process which can benefit greatly from the combined skills of creativity and planning.

Its relationship to advertising and other elements of the brand mix is key. It must achieve communication harmony often by taking on a complementary role. But getting it right will bring an exceptionally high return on marketing investment. It is not only a powerful medium, it is free.

THE WAY FORWARD

The agenda for packaging design, identified in this chapter, is of course changing all the time. Environmental pressures, backed up in some cases by legislation, will continue to move the goalposts just when you think you've lined up your shot. Meanwhile the forthcoming economic integration of the European Community will see unprecedented economies of scale as more and more products share the same technical specification.

The availability of a much wider range of goods in the shops will put additional pressure on packaging design to assist selection and promote brand charisma and personality in an ever-more-crowded market-place. The development of Eurobrands which cross national and cultural frontiers with ease will see the individual state of the art replacing the art of the individual state. As cross-border packaging becomes more prevalent than cross-border advertising, the Eurobrands will become the real arena – and true test – for active packaging.

However, Euro-marketeers may need to temper their enthusiasm for rationalised packaging. Remember that brands are like people, and people are individuals. 'This is my life, my town, my product' may be a stronger cry than central distribution and management.

Creativity and the Brand

GILES KEEBLE

Giles Keeble was educated at The King's School Canterbury and St John's College, Cambridge.

He joined JWT as an account manager in 1971, and then joined BMP as an account manager in 1973, working on Dry Cane, Southern Comfort, Saccone & Speed Wines, Cadbury's Smash, Tic Tac (Ferrero), Johnson & Johnson, and McOnomy Discount Stores.

He joined FGA as account manger in 1975, becoming a planner in 1976 and an account director in 1977, working on Smiths Crisps, Bulmers, Mettoy, Trumans, Wimpy Homes, Frazzles and Habitat. He then moved to the creative department, to become a copywriter. He joined Abbott Mead Vickers as a copywriter in 1979, working on Volvo, Paul Masson Wines, Time Out magazine, and British Bathrooms.

Giles joined WCRS as copywriter in 1981, and was elected to the board in 1985. He worked on BMW, Leicester Building Society, Hasselblad, Sharwoods, Duckham Oils, Qantas, Bass, Johnson's Wax, Taunton Cider, Laura Ashley, Wagon Wheels, DTI and Scotch Video Tape.

In 1985 he joined Leo Burnett as creative director.

Creativity and the Brand

GILES KEEBLE

Analysing 'creativity' is a bit like analysing a joke. It somehow misses the point. The process which leads to the production of an advertisement involves a lot of questions, from 'Who are we talking to?' and 'What are we trying to tell them?' to 'Where are we going to lunch?'

I'd like to start with another question before we consider the implications of what such-and-such a brand means to people and what that means to the advertising. It's a question that will already have been asked in this book, but I'd like to ask it again.

What *is* a brand?

According to the Oxford English Dictionary, it is (among other things) 'the mark made by a hot iron', a 'trade mark' (though not until 1827) and, as a verb, 'to mark indelibly as proof of ownership'.

As proof of ownership. The owner is saying 'This is mine', so other people will know 'That is his'.

Even today, a brand *name* often tells people who or where a product comes from. Cadbury's Dairy Milk, Heinz Baked Beans. But 'This is mine' isn't a guarantee of continued success. A product or a service with a brand name will only survive if customers continue to value it and buy it in preference to other products with other names.

An important shift has to take place: from the owner or manufacturer's 'This is mine', to the customer's 'This is mine'. The successful brand recognises the consumer. This is a crucial difference for advertising because, despite what many advertisers seem to believe, successful advertising is based on *response*. It is not based on the repetition of the brand name.

For a creative team, the 'desired response' is the starting point – or at least it should be. The question that should be asked is what does the brand mean to the consumer, not what it means to the client.

Understanding Brands

This is so fundamental it's worth a minor detour. It's crucial for good advertising, yet I believe it isn't fully appreciated by many clients and many of their agencies.

These are the people who believe that if you have a sophisticated product, all you have to do in their advertising is show sophisticated people enjoying your sophisticated brand. Or that you need someone in a food commercial to actually say 'Mmmm, it tastes good'. As Bill Bernbach said, 'The truth isn't the truth until someone believes you.'

The difference between stimulus and response was brought home to me about twenty years ago in an entertaining presentation made at JWT by Jeremy Bulmore and Stephen King. The bit I remember best went something like this:

> A man comes on to the stage and says to the audience 'I am funny' (Stimulus). The audience boos, hisses and throws rotten tomatoes at him (Response).

Compared to:

> A man comes on to the stage and tells a very funny joke (Stimulus). The audience laughs and thinks or says, 'He's funny' (Response).

Over the years, I've boiled this lesson down to a simple question to ask when you see a claim of any kind being made in an advertisement: 'Says who?'

There is often a world of difference between what an advertiser wants people to think and feel, and what they actually do think and feel. Where there is no difference, you'll probably find a successful brand. Where the difference is huge, either the brand has got problems or the agency has.

If the problem is the brand, advertising alone won't help. The product, the pack, the price may need looking at. Or the brand may be OK and the problem is that the client doesn't completely appreciate what the brand is, and the advertising reflects that lack of understanding. If the agency is compliant, it probably means dreadful advertising (I am not talking about effectiveness at this point. This is a subjective view.) If they aren't, it means hard work and a great deal of frustration.

On the other hand, there are times when the client knows what people think and feel, and would very much like to change those perceptions. Advertising is important, but it's the last step. Tesco could not have changed their 'pile 'em high, sell 'em cheap' image by advertising alone. There would have been a lot of 'dissonance'. They had to look first at the stores, the range of products and their packaging.

Long-term commitment to a change in brand identity.
The advertising could not come first.

Knowing where you are, where you'd like to be and how you can get there are vital to sustaining a successful brand. It starts with knowing the difference between the product you sell, and the brand your customer buys.

A PRODUCT, A BRAND

In writing about competitive effectiveness, Ted Levitt defines a brand somewhat differently from the dictionary.

> 'Competitive effectiveness demands that the successful seller offer his prospect and his customer more than the generic product itself. He must surround his product with a cluster of value satisfactions that differentiates his total offering from his competitors.'
> *(Theodore Levitt, The Marketing Mode).*

'A cluster of value satisfactions' is not a phrase you're likely to hear in a creative department. I suppose it means roughly the same as 'brand character', or 'brand identity', something that some people (not just in the creative department) understand intuitively but also something that can take time to understand.

A brand should have a guardian. For BMW, it was Robin Wight. Often an ad would be turned down, not because it wasn't good, but because it 'wasn't BMW'. What BMW is selling is more than a piece of machinery that will carry you from A to B. As Charles Revson of Revlon said: 'In the factory we make cosmetics. In the store we sell hope.'

Maybe it's easier to appreciate such a distinction for cosmetics than it is for some other product categories. There is certainly a view that where a product has a strong USP, there is less chance of a brand character being developed.

The Product and the USP

I believe a brand becomes a brand as soon it it comes in contact with a consumer. What the brand means to the consumer may not be what the manufacturer would like, so it makes sense to plan the nature of that contact. That's fine (but still not easy) for a new product, but much more difficult for an existing brand that needs a change of direction.

However, there are certain manufacturers who haven't bothered much about brand character at all, and it doesn't feature in their advertising.

Creativity and the Brand

Procter and Gamble are a classic example. They haven't bothered much because they have put their money and their energies elsewhere – into product superiority. Over the years, their success has been based on *demonstrably* better products. They have consistently spent more on research and development than their competitors.

When you have demonstrable product differences, it's easy to ignore brand character. Find the USP and bang it home. Don't knock it. Most creative people would love the chance to say something no one else can say.

The trouble with product differences is that other manufacturers catch up. The product differences get smaller, or disappear. The regulatory bodies (the ITVA or the FTC, for example) make it harder to claim what you might still be able to claim.

Let's take an example: Persil and Ariel. It seems to me that Persil has built a brand character over many years. Ariel is also a famous brand but it has no 'brand personality' – at least, not in any planned sense. (I'm sure it has a 'positioning'.) It became a brand as soon as people bought it, but its success was possibly based rather more on the product benefits than on brand personality, whereas Persil seems more of a mixture. I certainly know which advertising I prefer.

But just as you thought it was safe to switch on the telly, in 1989 along came Radion. From P&G, the begetters of Ariel? No. From Unilever, the begetters of Persil. A new USP: odours. No personality, just the product benefit backed by a lot of money. Very successful.

I don't known how it will all turn out, but the point I'd make is that if you have based your success on the *product*, what else do you have when someone comes along with something as good or better? I wonder where Radion will go when the other powders and liquids demonstrably cope with odours, too?

As I've said, it's much easier for a creative team to produce work when there *is* a USP, or at least a concrete proposition rather than an abstract one.

Creative people usually look for a point of difference. The important point is to make sure the point of difference is a relevant one. However, it's much more likely that the relevant point is shared by the competition. The trick is then to make it more *yours*, in some way, or to say it first. I've often heard a client say 'But anyone could say that' and the correct (though not always heeded) response has been 'Yes, but they *aren't* saying it.'

Heineken is a famous example. People were drinking lager instead of bitter because it was more refreshing. Amazingly, no one was saying it. Heineken took refreshment as its claim, and did it in a way that was impossible to copy, and was sustainable for years. Skol, I believe, responded with its own refreshment campaign. Which do you remember?

Here are two further examples, one which got it right and one which didn't.

On Scotch tape, Robin Wight discovered that you could re-record indefinitely without any loss of quality. He was told that this was equally true of other brands of tape, but they hadn't bothered with it. Robin came up with the idea of a lifetime guarantee, which led to some single-minded and extremely successful advertising.

Possibly flushed with this success, he turned to Varta batteries. The first problem was that nobody knew Varta made batteries, and when they did, they assumed they came from Bulgaria. The second problem was that the 'motivator' in the market was long life, and this was owned by Duracell. Robin came up with a leak-proof guarantee. But since people didn't think the batteries were any good in the first place, whether they leaked or not was totally irrelevant.

The idea that rescued Varta came from a proposition that had been staring everyone in the face. Varta are the best selling battery in Germany, a country quite well regarded for its technology. In test, the relaunch commercial moved awareness from an asterisk to 25 per cent.

IF IT AIN'T BROKE DON'T FIX IT

This is a piece of folklore that is often ignored. (Sometimes it should be ignored, but more of that later.) Creative teams often ignore it because of their own desire to 'come up with something new'.

Agencies ignore it because the client may put pressure on them to come up with something new. There is sometimes the suspicion that if they don't, they aren't earning their money.

Clients themselves ignore it when they are new brooms intent on indiscriminate sweeping. Schweppes lost a famous advertising property, I understand, for such a reason, though it was subsequently re-introduced.

These attitudes come from an understandable tendency to want to change things others have done: the 'Not Invented Here' syndrome. As Leo Burnett wrote 'Any fool can write a bad ad, but it takes a genius to keep his hands off a good one.'

When these changes occur, the agency or the client are worrying about themselves, rather than looking at the brand. We've all been guilty of this at some stage, but there are examples of continuity being preserved. At WCRS, we didn't ditch 'The Appliance of Science' for Zanussi; and most creative teams would be only too happy to carry on the good work on Heineken, Hamlet, or Carling Black Label.

'If it ain't broke don't fix it' is a sensible starting point if you're really interested in understanding the brand. But it is too often used as an excuse to avoid risk. Avoiding risk is, on the face of it, sensible too. But there must come a point when avoiding risk becomes a risk in itself.

Leo Burnett once quoted an American businessman who said 'I can't give you a formula for success. But I can give you a sure-fire formula for failure – just try to please everybody.' Or as Bill Bernbach put it: 'If you stand for something you will always find some people for you and some against you. If you stand for nothing, you will find nobody against you, and nobody for you.'

A brand needs a distinct identity, and preferably one that doesn't change too much. It may well be that it 'ain't broke'. It may be functioning perfectly well, but is it working as well as it could be? I'm sure this question is asked by many clients, but in those cases where the advertising is product-led, the question stops with the product, while the advertising, at least their type of advertising, stays the same. This can lead to discrepancies that I'm sure would horrify the client if they thought about them for a moment.

I saw a commercial recently that I know a certain client likes. The actresses in it are dubbed, and it is so obvious it's embarrassing. For me, that would be the equivalent of the packs being printed out of register. If *that* happened the client would be severely embarrassed. So it wouldn't happen. But they don't care about the professional quality of their advertising.

Clearly, some clients don't spend much thought on the 'totality' of a brand, or they aren't encouraged to. This may be genuine lack of interest, or it may be conditioned by the nature of the organisation. While it is the added value of the brands that keeps the company in profit, the consumer and what he or she thinks about the brands are a long way down the list of things to worry about. Although the advertising is usually the main contact the brand has with its customer, the agency is simply one of many suppliers.

A brand needs a guardian. But when it may need continuity of management, it is likely to have a new brand manager every few years, a new marketing director somewhat less frequently. When a brand may need refreshment (and the risks that will entail) it is being looked after on a day-to-day basis by people who can say 'No', but can't say 'Yes', whose main aim during their few years on the brand is to protect the status quo and their own behinds.

Even if the boat is sinking, don't rock it.

Nice Brand, Shame About the Ads

There are some very successful brands with dull unoriginal advertising: most detergents, most shampoos, many cereals, most coffee. Since clients, quite naturally, are interested in sales, this advertising must be associated with sales success or they wouldn't continue to run it.

In my naïvety, I can't believe that many of these clients – in their roles as human beings rather than product managers – wouldn't prefer advertising that is fresh and involving. The problem seems to be that they think it will have an adverse effect on sales.

Somewhere along the line they may have had their fingers burnt, for which agencies must accept some responsibility. But the argument I've heard, that creative people are interested in awards and not sales – even if it were true – can be defended on the grounds of being in the client's best interests.

Even the most formula-driven, product-led advertisers look for a point of difference. The point already made is that they tend to look for it in the product rather than the advertising. But so often, there is no difference in the product.

This is when an advertiser needs the best creative minds. The best advertising minds will understand the consumer, probably intuitively. He or she will dare to be different, will be willing to take risks, and will not talk down to the target audience.

If the client has a reputation for formula advertising, the best brains will not be interested, or not for long. A good salary is not the only motivation. If a client that believes in the power of advertising consistently demotivates the best brains, it is extremely bad business. It is a dismal fact (which of course will be denied in public) that many of the multinationals don't get the best brains, just the best bullshitters.

The key is the management and direction of the most original brains. The client and the agency managements have a duty to agree a strategy, a strategy that can be boiled down to a single purpose, with one proposition, not three or four. If this part of the process can be handled properly, then it is easier to create ideas and easier to judge whether the ideas are on strategy.

The differences between the creative team and the client are often over the execution rather than the strategy, over doing something fresh rather than to a formula. The 'Twins' commercial for Biactol is a Proctor and Gamble formula, but in this case they allowed the execution and, more important, the *tone* of it to be totally fresh.

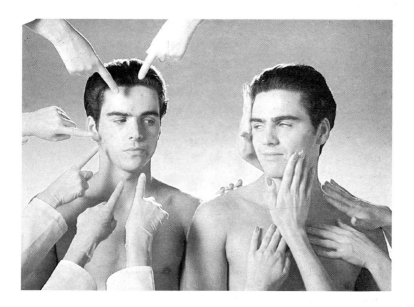

Formula advertising doesn't all have to look the same

The real challenge for an agency and an advertiser is to create a strong brand identity when there are no discernible or relevant product differences. This is where clients and agencies who *only* look for a USP, or only accept product-based advertising, go astray.

I remember having a conversation with such a client who conceded that there was undoubtedly a place in effective advertising for developing 'brand character'. They also conceded that they had no way, within their tried and tested methodologies, of arriving at it.

A creative brief must be allowed to accept that there is no USP or demonstrable difference. It must be structured so that it forces the whole team (client included) to look at the *response* that is wanted from the advertising, not just the stimulus, and to look at it in a variety of ways. Will the response be rational? Will it be sensual (touch, taste, smell, sight)? Will it be emotional? Or a mixture of all three?

If the future of a brand's advertising is only based on accepted formulas (that is, what has been done in the past) at least two risks are being taken. One is that your brand may not be as successful as it could be. Another is that a competitor might become more relevant and more appealing.

Similarly, it is quite sensible to ask the question, 'Since this worked so well in Guatamala, I wonder if it will work equally well over here?' (If the answer is thought to be yes, a creative department is not needed – just an account manager and a producer.)

It is also possible that if someone spends all their time looking over their shoulder at what they've done in the past, they may eventually walk into a lamppost.

OPTIONS AND OPPORTUNITIES

A strong culture can be an important part of success, but for continued survival, an organisation must have the ability to change, even change dramatically. Someone, somewhere has to keep asking the question 'Why are we doing what we are doing?' The answer shouldn't be 'because that's what we've always done.'

The 'someone' might be a client, or it might be one of the agency team. The questioning should be part of a continuous assessment. The round of 'Where are we? Where could we be? How do we get there? Where are we?' (Occasionally, the most apt response to 'How do we get there?' is the Spike Milligan response, 'If I were you I wouldn't be starting from here'.)

This continuous evaluation will take into consideration the consumer and the competition in the most complete sense, and will help make those important decisions that affect not just the advertising, but the product formulation and the packaging: decisions not to fix, or to evolve, to bring back or to change.

Here are some examples of brands that I believe have followed those options.

Not fixed: Cadbury's Milk Tray. The pack's been updated, but the advertising idea hasn't been touched.

Evolution: Oxo. A continuous process of updating.

Bring back: Schweppes and Arthur for Kattomeat. Two examples of brand properties that lived on even when the advertising had stopped.

Change: Red Mountain Coffee. A refreshing change, not just for the brand, but for the market.

So many products come and go, the overall feeling may be one of continuous flux. But when a brand property has been built up, it takes a long time to die.

A point to bear in mind also is that long-lasting brand properties have had millions of pounds invested in them – the kind of exposure that just can't be bought any more (unless you're the government selling off an industry. Sid will be remembered, I'm afraid, for quite a while.)

So if you've got a brand property, make sure it's had its day before you get rid of it. You might be able to do something very fresh with it. Gordon's Gin is an interesting case. It's a fresh execution built around an old property, the green bottle, a property the client temporarily relinquished. It was no accident that Sainsbury's own-label and White Satin adopted green bottles for themselves.

Where Do You Start?

Often a creative team will be working on an existing campaign, where the rules and the guidelines have been set. However, every now and then we will get the chance to do something completely different. This opportunity might arise from a pitch, or because of a change of management, or the success of the competition.

Whenever I look at a brief, I try to look for an idea that is campaignable. What I'm also after is something that rings true. A brand, as has been pointed out, only exists in the mind of the consumer. It is a mixture of emotional, rational, and physical reactions to the product, its name, it packaging, its price and so on.

The starting point for the advertising is to find a way to the heart of the brand and find something there that can be dramatised. This may just be an emotional response, or it may be a rational one.

For example, when Ken Hoggins and I worked on Wagon Wheels, it was the size of the biscuit (which is also its USP). This eventually led to 'What a Mouthful', based on a character who had a mouth big enough to eat a Wagon Wheel 'in one delicious bite'. (Interestingly, before the advertising ran, the client had to improve the quality of the biscuit, which had deteriorated over the years. Giving people more of something they don't particularly like isn't really a benefit.)

Although the ad turned out to be a one-off, it *was* a campaign idea. I was sad not to be able to develop it. I notice that the client has since returned to covered wagons and the Wild American West. (Our research suggested this was irrelevant to today's kids). Since this is where the brand started, you could say the wheel has turned full circle.

THE IMPORTANCE OF CAMPAIGNS

Where there's a brand property, there's a campaign.

On winning a top award for the John Smith's Bitter campaign, John Webster remarked that anyone worth their salt should be able to do a good one-off ad from time to time; the hard thing to do is to come up with a great campaign. Campaigns are the life-blood of a brand, and therefore of the advertiser's business (and of the agency's business, for that matter).

When you have a good campaign, everything is easier – the next ad in the series, the trade ad, the point of sale, the sales conference. There's a theme everyone can share – the advertiser and his employees, the agency *and* the customer.

Customers like to feel a campaign is *their* campaign. That's true of Milk Tray, it's true of Perrier, and it's probably true of Carling Black Label. When you have a great campaign you'll see less of the 'not invented here' problem. Possibly more creative people have become famous continuing great campaigns like Heineken and Hamlet than by starting one themselves.

The secret is to keep a campaign fresh, which includes keeping it relevant. Bernbach wrote:

> 'Live in the current idiom and you will create in it. If you follow and enjoy and are excited by the new traits in art, in writing, in industry, in personal relationships... whatever you do will naturally be of today.'

Sometimes circumstances change so much that campaigns die. Hamlet has been lost to anti-tobacco regulations. (Smoking even kills ads.) At the time of writing Heineken has changed for reasons I don't fully understand. Certainly the lager market has changed a great deal since the campaign first appeared. Perhaps Heineken's humorous position in the market has been usurped by Carling Black Label. (If so, it's an interesting switch. Carling's campaign thought was never in the same league as Heineken's, but the execution of it has been considerably refreshed over the past few years. Also, I know from personal experience that a lot of candidate Carling scripts would have been better Heineken ideas. Give that squirrel a Heineken then cut to the Carling film....)

If we can accept that campaigns *are* important, why aren't there more of them? I think there are a number of reasons.

Cost

Not many advertisers can afford either the media budget or the production budget to run more than one film. However, if you are lucky enough to get a campaign idea, think hard about how it can be developed. Look at time lengths, media choice, even point of sale. Try to come at the consumer from different directions.

When a team comes up with a campaignable idea, I like to see more than one script, even if we've only been asked for one. It helps me see that the campaign can work, and it helps the client see they're buying something that has 'legs', something that's an investment.

New Brooms

This point has been made about established advertising being changed when it ought not to have been. It applies equally to killing off a campaign before it has got into its stride. (This could be a new creative director as well as a new client.)

Formula Advertising

I need to make a quick distinction here between an advertiser running more than one commercial and what I mean by a campaign. I mean that the commercials or press ads in a campaign find *different* ways of reaching the same conclusion, and are not simply a similar execution with minor differences (such as a man presenter as well as a woman).

A true campaign allows a brand to develop its personality. Freshness can accompany familiarity. It keeps it alive. The relationship a consumer has with a brand can be a bit like a marriage – it needs a little spontaneity to stop the two partners taking each other for granted.

Copies and repetitions of a formula bore and stultify, even though they may protect share. And because the consumer *as person* rather than as customer is neglected, the advertiser needs to rely on spend rather than involvement: the stimulus rather than the response.

Formula advertising *can* produce great work. After all, Heineken is a classic 'Before and After'. In the hands of some clients (assuming they would have bought it in the first place), after the first commercial of policemen's feet in need of refreshment, the second commercial would have been postmen's feet.

If the client culture is to minimise risk by *repeating* success, campaigns become almost impossible and creative departments practically redundant. Because when one commercial has worked in the market place, the next in the series must be as similar as possible, just in case the things that are changed are the things that affect the sale. (I can understand this for direct response advertising. As Ogilvy said, 'If you are lucky enough to write a good advertisement, repeat it until it stops pulling.' On the whole, brand advertising is about larger issues, such as maintaining share.)

The thinking, where there are formulae, is all *retrospective;* whereas developing a brand, and a campaign of advertising to go with it, looks *forward* to the possibilities.

The Slide Rule Rules

Research has its place, but it is so often used without question that it can do more damage than good. As Ogilvy said nearly *thirty* years ago, 'I notice increasing reluctance on the part of marketing executives to use judgement: they are coming to rely too much on research and they use it as a drunkard uses a lamppost, for support rather than for illumination.'

Even Ted Levitt of the 'cluster of value satisfactions' fame, argues that the human rule is more important than the slide rule, even when selling a slide rule. Brands are a blend of different appeals, and good advertising reflects that blend.

An ad can depend on a gesture or a look. How do you put that on a storyboard? (Try putting the original Cointreau commercial on a storyboard.) A campaign can depend on a tone of voice. How do you measure that on a five-point normative scale?

A successful brand recognizes the consumer. So should its advertising. Instead, it so often perpetuates the myth of the perfect family, mother, lover, experience, etc. Watch people eating. Do they smile each time they take a bite? Now watch some food commercials.

Some of the people, I'm afraid, will fall for it some of the time. And if you have a good product and patronising advertising, the product will continue to do well. But could it do better?

Lack of Time and Talent

It can take time to come up with a great idea. Advertising is a business of deadlines, so there isn't always enough time. 'Do you want it now or do you want it great?' can be the refuge of laziness. But where there is a modicum of trust, an agency should be allowed more time to get it great. The Whitbread client allowed CDP more time on Heineken – a lot more time.

However, more time won't help when there's a lack of talent. Much of our advertising is second rate. When it's on strategy, it's often boring, and sometimes when its not boring it's off strategy. There are too few ideas, too little an understanding of the consumer.

This is not always the client's fault. Often the creative brief is a useless starting point. Often the creative team has little curiosity about the product or its customers. To them, being 'creative' means ripping off a new (or old) joke, or a video technique, or a sequence from a film before anyone else does. This in itself will lead nowhere. (This is not to say that borrowing an idea can't lead to great advertising. It depends what the idea is, how relevant it is, and what you do with it.)

Let us assume that, against all odds, the work is good. There are further hurdles. The ITVA (much more preferable than government legislation, but often serving God and Mammon). Research. The ability of the account group to sell the work (or their ability to make sure it doesn't get through).

Advertising is a relatively simple business, made difficult by people trying too hard to justify themselves (or their salaries). *Great* work of any kind is always hard, and needs an array of different talents. Client and agency: it all comes down to the quality of people.

BRANDS ARE A PART OF PEOPLE'S LIVES

This is really the whole simple point. Brands fit into people's lives in ways that many advertisers and some agencies don't seem to understand. People have relationships with their brands, and the advertising is perhaps (along with the packaging) the most visible point of contact.

Bernbach wrote: 'To succeed, an ad (or a person or a product for that matter) must establish its own unique personality, or it will never be noticed.' You will not find the essence of that personality in usage and image studies, nor even in group discussions (though you're more likely to get insights from the latter).

You'll find it by observing the world and how people live, how they experience things, how they communicate with each other, their loves and their hatreds, their prejudices and superstitions, their kindness and sentiment and their senses of humour.

If you aren't interested in these things, in any business, you don't deserve to succeed. And eventually, God willing, you won't.

A client I worked for once said 'I don't care what people think of my advertising.' I replied 'If that's what you really think, don't ever tell the creative department.'

Sadly, his customers already know.

Brand Valuation

MICHAEL BIRKIN

Michael Birkin is a graduate of University College London, where he studied law. He became a chartered accountant at Price Waterhouse where he began his career before becoming personal assistant to Sir Mark Weinberg, the chairman of Allied Dunbar. He took up his present position as group chief executive of Interbrand Group plc in January 1987.

Interbrand is the world's leading consultancy in the area of branding, with offices in London, New York, Los Angeles, Chicago, Hamburg and Tokyo, Milan and Sydney.

Michael was one of the architects of the methodology for valuing brands, and he has unequalled experience in the practice of brand valuation. As well as being a frequent speaker at major conferences, he has also contributed to Brand Valuation: Establishing a True and Fair View, *published by Hutchinson Business Books, and* Brand and Goodwill Accounting Strategies, *published by Woodhead-Faulkner Limited.*

CHAPTER EIGHT

Brand Valuation

MICHAEL BIRKIN

In 1984 News Group, the Australian flagship company of Rupert Murdoch's world-wide publishing empire, included a valuation for 'publishing titles' in its balance sheet. Murdoch did this because the 'goodwill' element of publishing acquisitions – the difference between the value of the tangible net assets and the price paid – can be enormous, and, being an acquisitive company, the goodwill write-offs which his company was being forced to take were ravaging his balance sheet. He well knew that much of the 'goodwill' he was buying comprised the publishing titles; he therefore placed a value on these and included this valuation in the balance sheet. This simple procedure restored his balance sheet, solved many of the problems of goodwill write-offs, and dramatically reduced gearing. Indeed, without this balance sheet valuation of publishing titles, it is unlikely that Murdoch would have been able to expand his business by acquisition, particularly in the US.

Reckitt and Colman was faced with exactly the same problem in 1985, having acquired Airwick Industries from Ciba-Geigy. It capitalised the value of the Airwick brand, for if it had not done so its net assets would have been reduced considerably.

Next in line was the mighty Grand Metropolitan. This company acquired Heublein in 1987, and Heublein's main asset was the Smirnoff brand. In August 1988 Grand Metropolitan announced that a large part of the sum it paid for Heublein was attributable to the Smirnoff brand, and it would therefore not write this off but, rather, would include acquired brands in its balance sheet at a sum of £588m. Not until later in the year did observers realise that this move was a trailer to the massive $5.5bn Pillsbury bid, successfully concluded in January 1989.

The News Group, Reckitt and Colman and Grand Metropolitan brand valuations and other valuations in the publishing industry went largely unremarked. Observers did not altogether realise that publishing titles were in fact brands (the phrase 'publishing title' has a certain weightiness to it). However, what really put the cat among the accounting pigeons was the decision of Rank Hovis McDougall PLC (RHM) to value all its brands, acquired and otherwise, and to place this valuation in its balance sheet. News of this valuation broke in late November 1988, and debate has raged ever since. This valuation was conducted in conjunction with Interbrand Group plc, the specialist international branding consultancy.

Since RHM valued its brands, many major UK quoted companies, including Guinness, United Biscuits, Cadbury-Schweppes and Lonrho, have included brand valuations in their balance sheets, though mainly for acquired brands only – Guinness, for example, announced a £1.7bn valuation of brands acquired in the previous four years. In France, too, BSN has placed acquired brands on its balance sheet. Many more companies have valued their brands, but not used the valuations for balance sheet purposes. Rather, they have been more concerned with brand management, strategy, brand licensing, and with the valuation of brands for taxation and merger and acquisition purposes.

The phenomenon of brand valuation has also spread way beyond Britain, France and Australia. In the US, for example, the issue of how brand equities can be defined, measured and managed has become, according to one observer, 'the hottest topic in marketing today'. Even Japanese business is taking an interest – overseas acquisitions by Japanese companies are increasingly taking place in the branded goods field, where much of the acquired value is intangible. Japanese companies are as keen as any others to evaluate the worth of the intangible assets they are acquiring.

ALTERNATIVE WAYS TO VALUE BRANDS

The fundamental problem when valuing brands is that there is no 'open market' for these assets. When corporations or residential properties are valued, the market provides a solid starting point for the valuation exercise. The market value of a brand, on the other hand, is simply the price which a particular purchaser is prepared to pay. A system has been developed, therefore, which values a brand on the basis of its value to its current owner – the 'existing use' valuation. This system, which is consistent with the way in which assets such as industrial buildings are valued, is well explained in the 1988 Rank Hovis McDougall PLC report and accounts:

'This basis of valuation ignores any possible alternative use of a brand, any possible extension to the range of products currently marketed under a brand, any element of hope value and any possible increase of value of a brand due to either a special investment or a financial transaction (eg licensing) which would leave the Group with a different interest from the one being valued.'

When developing an 'existing use' methodology, a variety of possible methods were explored for valuing brands.

Premium Pricing

Such a valuation is based upon the extra price (or profit) which a branded product may command over an unbranded or generic equivalent. However, the major benefits which branded products offer to manufacturers often relate to security and stability of future demand, and effective utilisation of assets, rather than to premium pricing, so premium pricing is rarely an acceptable method of brand valuation. A strong brand which the retailer must stock due to customer demand also provides its owner with a platform for the sale of additional products. At a practical level, it should be remembered as well that many branded products (for example most perfumes) have no generic equivalents and, in many instances (eg the Mars Bar) it is difficult to conceive that a generically-equivalent product could be offered at anything like as keen a price as the branded product. Furthermore, price is often manipulated to achieve short-term share advantage, a practice which would have profound consequences for any methodology based upon this concept. Therefore the value of a brand clearly cannot be determined by premium pricing alone; rather evidence of a strong price premium is an indication of brand strength.

Esteem

There have been moves, particularly in the United States, to develop brand valuation methodologies based principally on measures of brand recognition, esteem or awareness. Although the Interbrand metholodology recognises that top-of-mind brand awareness can at times be critical to a brand's success (and is therefore a factor in assessing the overall strength of the brand), to build a model using as its corner-stone such 'soft' measures is simply unrealistic.

Historical Cost

As balance sheets are traditionally drawn up on an historical cost basis, it was necessary to look at ways to value brands based upon the aggregate of all marketing, advertising and research and development expenditure devoted to the brand over a period of time. This approach however, was rejected quite quickly; if the value of a brand is a function of the cost of its development, failed brands may well be attributed high values, and skilfully managed, powerful and profitable brands with modest budgets would be undervalued.

Discounted Cash Flow

The concept of using discounted cash flow (DCF) techniques to achieve a brand valuation is attractive. Strong brands are, in effect, a form of annuity to their owners, so any system which can accurately assess the value of future cash flows is entirely supportable. The problem of DCF lies in its sensitivity: wide fluctuations can arise from relatively minor shifts in inflation and/or interest rate assumptions; this fact, coupled with the range of cash flows which can result from the differing brand development assumptions, means that DCF is a somewhat difficult tool to use in the brand valuation area. Even when these difficulties can be overcome, the valuer has the practical problem that he is generally given little time to complete the valuation, and often has to satisfy auditors. In such a situation, modelling techniques using DCF are very hard to apply. Notwithstanding this, the Interbrand approach detailed below has been adapted to value brands on a DCF basis.

THE NORMAL APPROACH

The approach adopted by Interbrand (and by far the most frequently used system) is an earnings multiple system; ie an appropriate multiple is applied to the true earnings of the brand. Conceptually the system is sound (the conceptual arguments which support a discounted cash flow system apply equally to an earnings multiple system) and, practically, the system is robust, auditable and the valuation can be completed in a short time-frame, provided always that the requisite marketing, financial and trademark legal skills are harnessed. The system also has the not inconsiderable advantage that hard, proven data is used which is verifiable.

To determine a brand's value, then, certain key factors need to be determined:

- brand earnings (or cash flows);
- brand strength (which determines the relative size of the multiple or discount rate);
- the range of the multiples (or discount rates).

Brand Earnings

A vital factor in determining the value of a brand is its profitability or potential profitability, particularly its profitability over time. However, to arrive at a balance sheet value it is not enough merely to apply a simple multiplier to post-tax profits. First, not all of the profitability of a brand can necessarily be applied to the valuation of that brand. A brand may be essentially a commodity product, or may gain much of its profitability from its distribution system. The elements of profitability which do not result from the brand's identity must therefore be exluded. This is achieved through both careful analysis of the financial performance and an assessment of those critical factors which contribute to the strength of the brand.

Second, the valuation itself may be materially affected by using a single, possibly unrepresentative year's profit. For this reason, a smoothing element should be introduced; generally, a three-year weighted average of historical profits is used.

The following must be taken into consideration in calculating brand earnings:

Determining brand profits: Since it is the worth of the brand to the business which is being valued, it is important that the profit on which this valuation is based is clearly defined. For balance sheet purposes this profit must be the fully absorbed profit of the brand after allocation of central overhead costs, but before interest charges. Taxation is of course also deducted, as will be explained later. For the purposes of evaluating the brand, interest costs are ignored since the basis of funding chosen for the brand is irrelevant to the brand's performance. Were interest to be included in the calculation, the valuation could be materially affected by changes in corporate financing arrangements. As such arrangements are generally not brand-related they are normally excluded when determining profit.

The elimination of own-label profits: The profits to which an earnings multiple is applied must relate only to the brand being valued, and not to other, unbranded goods which may be produced in parallel with the brand but which are not sold under the brand name.

These profits may be separately identified by the company through its accounting systems; alternatively, judgement may need to be exercised in assessing the extent of such profits, based on production volumes, sales values or other acceptable methods. Insofar as 'allocation' is at the heart of much accountancy, the elimination of own-label profits has been found to be entirely feasible.

The compounding of historical profits to present-day values: Since historical earnings form the basis of the valuation, these values must be adapted to present-day figures by adjustments for inflation. This has the effect of ensuring that performance is reviewed at constant levels.

The weighting of historical earnings: Weighting is applied to historical earnings so as to determine a prudent and conservative level of ongoing profitability to which to apply an appropriate multiple. Thus once historical profits have been adjusted to present-day values, a weighting factor must be allocated to each year's brand profits which is representative of the degree of importance appropriate for that particular year. In many cases a simple weighting of three times for the current year, twice for the previous year and once for the year before that is used. These aggregate earnings are then divided by the sum of the weighting factors used.

Provision for decline: There is a basic accounting rule that benefits should only be taken when they are earned, but that losses should be provided for as soon as they are known. This rule further requires that future brand profitability is reviewed so as to see whether the profits on which the valuation is based will be maintained. Where the weighted average historical earnings are clearly below the forecast brand profits in future years, no provision for decline is necessary. However, it may be necessary to review the weighting allocation if forecast future earnings are significantly in excess of the weighted average profit value, and are expected to remain at this level in the foreseeable future. The reason is that historical profits may have been depressed by factors now brought under control, and it may be appropriate therefore to place greater reliance on more recent earnings when arriving at a valuation. Where the weighted average earnings are greater than the forecast future brand profits, a provision for decline may be necessary to reflect the reduced level of future profitability.

Remuneration of capital: Having established the weighted average profits for the brand and confirmed that this level of profitability will continue for the foreseeable future, the elements of these profits that result from the brand have to be separated out from non-brand-related elements. For example, the profits accruing from a branded bread product will comprise the normal profits which would be made from the production of unbranded bread plus the extra profits generated through branded product activities. There are several ways of identifying and eliminating product-related profit, but the most frequently used system is that of charging the capital tied up in the production of the brand with a return one might expect to achieve if one was simply selling a generic.

Whichever method is chosen, the following factors must be taken into account (although their importance will vary significantly depending upon the product area in which the brand operates):

- The volume enjoyed by a branded product is normally directly related to the use of a brand. A generic or unbranded equivalent would normally command neither the volume nor the stablity of demand of the branded product.
- Much of the brand's profitability will come from economies of scale brought about by this extra volume and by stability of demand.
- The brand may in certain instances be sold at a price premium, perhaps a substantial premium, to a generic or unbranded equivalent. Some of this premium may be used to support the advertising investment, but in any event there may well be an enhanced profit contribution.

Each of these factors must be considered before the assessment of brand-related earnings can be made. In addition, there may be special factors relating to the particular brand under review.

Taxation: The multiples which we use are applied to the brand's post-tax profit figures. Therefore it is vital that all the reported earnings are collected on the same basis. A tax rate is applied which is generally the medium-term effective tax rate forecast for the company.

Brand Strength

The determination of the multiple (or discount rate, in the case of DCF valuations) to be applied to brand profit is derived from an in-depth assessment of brand strength. This requires a detailed review of each brand, its positioning, the market in which it operates, competition, past performance, future plans, and risks to the brand.

The brand strength is a composite of seven weighted factors, each of which is scored according to clearly established and consistent guidelines. These key factors are as follows:

- *Leadership*. A brand which leads its market sector is a more stable and valuable property than a brand lower down the order.
- *Stability*. Long-established brands which command consumer loyalty and have become part of the 'fabric' of their markets are particularly valuable.
- *Market*. Brands in markets such as food and drinks are intrinsically more valuable than brands in, for example, high-tech or clothing areas, since these latter markets are more vulnerable to technological or fashion changes.
- *Internationality*. International brands are inherently more valuable than national, regional or local brands.
- *Trend*. The overall long-term trend of the brand is an important measure of its ability to remain contemporary and relevant to consumers, and hence of its value.
- *Support*. Those brand names which have received consistent investment and focused support must be regarded as more valuable than those which have not. While the amount spent in supporting a brand is important, the quality of this support is equally significant.
- *Protection*. A registered trademark is a statutory monopoly in a name, device, or combination of these two. Other protection may exist in common law, at least in certain countries. The strength and breadth of the brand's protection is critical in assessing its worth.

The brand is scored for each of these factors according to different weightings, and the resultant total, known as the 'brand strength score', is expressed as a percentage. Clearly the higher the percentage, the higher the multiple which should be applied to the brand earnings. (In a DCF valuation, the higher the score the lower the discount rate and greater the period of years used in the model.)

The Range of Multiples

In fixing the multiples to be applied to brand profits as a result of the brand strength assessment, the closest available analogy to the return from a notional perfect brand is the return from an entirely risk-free investment. However, the perfect brand does not operate in a risk-free environment, and the return from a risk-free investment is capital-free, while part of a brand's earnings results from the capital employed in producing the product. Allowances for these factors must be made in determining the multiple to be applied to a brand operating in a real business environment. Thus the highest multiple that can be applied will be somewhat lower than that for a risk-free investment, and may vary from business to business and industry to industry.

The price–earnings ratios of strongly-branded industry sectors also provide an indication of the multiples that can reasonably be considered to apply to brands for balance sheet purposes; thus the multiples at the high end of the scale should be greater than the average P/E ratio of the sector in which the company operates, and those at the low end of the scale will be below this ratio. In practice, the multiple which the Interbrand methodology normally attributes to a notional 'perfect brand' is twenty times average annual brand-related earnings, though the multiple attributed to an 'average' brand is substantially lower than this.

THE EFFECTS OF PUTTING BRANDS ON THE BALANCE SHEET

Within the context of the protracted and meandering balance sheet debate, brand valuation has burst on the scene as a form of 'pre-emptive' strike by frustrated owners of valuable assets with real balance sheet problems. It is, however, just one of several moves to influence the basis of current accounting, albeit within current accounting rules. Brands, however, have one key difference from many other intangible assets – they are identifiable, separable pieces of legal property which are increasingly bought and sold independently from the other assets of the business.

What, then, motivates companies to capitalise their brands?

Goodwill

Though the balance sheet debate has recently gained particular momentum, the question as to how a company should account for purchased goodwill has been a concern for much longer.

Purchased goodwill is simply the difference between the price paid for a company and the value of the underlying net assets at the date of purchase. The current use accounting rules (SSAP 22) require a company to account for purchased goodwill in one of two ways:

1. To capitalise goodwill as an intangible asset and to depreciate the amount through the profit and loss account of the company

over such period of years as the company and its auditors consider reasonable; or

2. To write off the whole goodwill amount against the reserves of the company at the date of purchase.

Under either treatment it is clearly in the company's interest to minimise the goodwill figure. The first approach is now rarely followed in the UK, however, as the effect of it is to depress profits and hence earnings per share. However, this policy becomes much more attractive if part of the goodwill is properly attributed to brands that have been in existence for many years and which can be found to be appreciating in value, rather than depreciating.

In this instance a large part of the 'goodwill' element in the acquisition can be placed on the balance sheet and only the small 'rump' depreciated.

If the latter policy is adopted (write-off against reserves) brand valuations can materially reduce the amount needing to be written off as the brand values are retained on the balance sheet; in this way acquisitive companies can maintain reasonable balance sheet profiles.

It must be said, however, that the brands being valued should be sufficiently strong that there are no grounds for depreciating these assets – declining brand values would leave the company with the same problem as it set out with.

Gearing

It follows from the policy of writing off purchased goodwill on acquisition that gearing ratios are inevitably adversely affected. Despite the fact that many banks claim to lend primarily on the basis of interest cover, the reality for most businesses is still somewhat different – not only does good interest cover have to be proven, but full security is sought over assets, and gearing ratios are closely watched. Therefore not to undertake a brand valuation exercise on the acquistion of valuable brands potentially puts a company in an inappropriately inflexible position.

Stock Exchange Rules

The Stock Exchange issued a statement in January 1989 stating that brands qualified as assets, for calculating whether a Class 1 circular is required to be sent to the shareholders of a company on the acquisiton of another business, provided they were properly valued and provided too that they were actually included in the balance sheet (a simple note to the accounts would not suffice).

The take-over rules in the UK require a company to issue such a circular seeking shareholder approval, should the purchase price of its target be in excess of 25 per cent of the net assets of the acquiring company. Seeking such approval is intended as a protection for shareholders, but it much reduces flexibility and responsiveness when making acquisitions, particularly when there is a competitive situation – the vendor would clearly prefer to deal with an acquirer who can give a firm decision without the need to ballot shareholders.

Furthermore if the company has a hostile shareholder on its register, it may find difficulty in getting a decison, without granting other concessions.

Over recent years the problem has developed for acquisitive companies that by writing off goodwill as acquired, their net assets have been reduced, therefore increasing the likelihood that Class 1 circulars are required for even relatively small acquisitions. The Stock Exchange class tests were never intended to be triggered in such instances, and brand valuations therefore enable companies to preserve their balance sheets while retaining flexibility. This single factor has proved a key stimulus to companies to capitalise brand values on their balance sheets.

Borrowing Capabilities

Banks in the UK are beginning to look at brands as assets on which they can secure borrowings. Moreover, in certain instances where brand valuations are not being used for security, appropriate valuations provide an argument for reduced coupon rates. It should be said that this benefit is only now starting to gain acceptance; however, the fact that brands are separable and identifiable pieces of legal property is important to lenders.

OTHER APPLICATIONS OF BRAND VALUATION

While accountants wrestle with the thorny issues of accounting for intangible assets and the nature of the balance sheet, the fact that brands have become more widely recognised as specific assets of great worth, and the fact too that robust, verifiable tools have been developed to measure that worth, has led to new applications for brand valuation, evaluation and audit techniques which go way beyond the somewhat narrow, technical balance sheet debate.

These new measurement and evaluation techniques are now being used in a number of new areas including:

Acquistions, Disposals and Mergers

Around the world we are seeing brands being bought and sold at an increasing rate, reflecting the heightened awareness of brands as major assets and recognition of the true worth of companies with strong brand portfolios. Not surprisingly, the prices being paid even today for brands are well ahead of those considered possible five or ten years ago. Brand valuation can provide dramatic insights into the quality and potential of brand assets, and is used extensively to help in negotiations on brand transactions. Brand valuation can also be an invaluable tool in situations involving contested bids (normally on behalf of the threatened company which feels that the acquiror has not fully appreciated the value of its assets).

Investor Relations

There is currently a distinct preference among investors to invest money in companies with quality (ie secure) earnings, rather than in companies that are more entrepreneurially orientated. Strong brands can provide the quality of earnings that investors are looking for, and a brand valuation report may give investors considerable comfort with regard to the underlying quality of earnings of a branded goods business.

Brand Licensing and Franchising

It is very difficult to negotiate appropriate royalty rates for a brand unless the true value of the brand being licensed is known. Historically, companies have been reluctant to set realistic royalties. A brand valuation adds weight and substance to any party wishing to negotiate a more realistic royalty rate.

Tax Planning

Internal brand licensing between a brand owner and its overseas subsidiaries can be extremely tax efficient, and a brand valuation can be essential in persuading local tax authorities that the license constitutes a true transfer of value.

Brand Management

Measuring a brand's performance entails far more than merely looking at market size. A brand evaluation exercise necessitates a comprehensive audit of the brand portfolio, which in turn leads to insights as to each brand's strengths and weaknesses and those areas of brand husbandry that require attention. There are a number of specific situations under this heading where a brand valuation exercise helps clarify the issues considerably.

Brand strategy: The evaluation of a portfolio of brands accurately assesses those brands which have a logic to the proprietor, and those that do not. It is vital for a brand owner to constantly review his portfolio, to make sure he can afford to appropriately support the range. Brand evaluation shows which brands are being neglected, and points to those brands which will have a greater value to another party. Equally, the exercise shows where the brand owner should consider further acquisitions to consolidate the strength of his existing brands.

Resource allocation: One of the vexed issues of business today is how to spread limited marketing resources across a range of brands. Historically, such allocations have been determined through an arbitrary budgeting process, following the normal battle between the 'shoot from the hip' marketeers and the 'penny-pinching' accountants. Brand evaluation clearly and systematically points to where the money is needed most, and helps the brand owner to avoid either spreading his overall spend too thinly, or pushing his budget in the wrong direction.

Brand extension: It is estimated that perhaps 19 out of every 20 new brands fail; such an attrition rate is horrendous, and 'stretching' an existing brand may therefore be a more sensible strategy than attempting to develop a new brand from scratch. It is virtually impossible, for example, to get a new food brand into national distribution in most developed countries without a multi-million dollar advertising budget – major retailers simply cannot be persuaded to stock a new brand without a large promotional budget, and without the support of the major retailers any new brand is doomed. The problem remains, however, to determine which brands are capable of being 'stretched' without losing their key brand equity. Although it is trite (and indeed empirically incorrect) to say brands with greater value have more development potential than those with lesser value, nonetheless the brand strength analysis brings out a brand's core values upon which one can build, and reduces the risks of getting it wrong.

Geographical expansion: In today's markets, being international can be hugely advantageous. The opportunities for further growth and the economies of scale one can achieve by crossing borders makes a 'global' strategy most attractive. However, not all brands will travel and, as for brand extension, the costs of international development are massive. (A by no means comprehensive catalogue of costs would include initial research and development; market research; distribution; training sales forces; initial advertising and promotion; design costs; and brand auditing and accounting.) Companies cannot afford to get it wrong, and as good brand evaluation work will always assess a brand's geographical capability, many lessons can be learned before they become expensive mistakes.

Good brand husbandry: The evaluation exercise also stimulates dialogue between marketing and financial management – something lacking in most companies – with the result that marketing managers become more aware of brands as financial assets, and financial managers more aware of brands as marketing assets. Brand valuation should prevent brands being used as training grounds for young brand managers; rather their good and creative ideas should be controlled from a higher level, from where they can be used as a part of a longer-term strategy.

CONCLUSION

Although the issue of 'brands on the balance sheet' remains the most publicised aspect of brand valuation, I have tried to show that its other applications offer an enduring benefit to brand owners. At this stage the concept is still young, yet it seems set to increase in importance as brands are recognised as the secure cash flow generating properties that they are.

CHAPTER NINE

Multinational Brand Marketing

CHRISTINE RESTALL

A graduate of University College London, Christine Restall has worked in many consumer goods markets on a multinational basis, both in market research and in advertising. After training at SH Benson, she become research manager at Allied Breweries in 1970. She then moved to Ogilvy & Mather and on to McCann-Erickson, with seven years as European strategic planning director and four as UK executive planning director. She joined The Research Business International in 1989.

Multinational Brand Marketing

CHRISTINE RESTALL

THE PRESSURE ON COMPANIES TOWARDS INTERNATIONAL MARKETING

Once a certain size and maturity is reached, most companies find themselves forced to look beyond their original country borders for growth, because of saturated home markets. The initial impetus to export has usually come from the need for growth. Having achieved greater mass, the corporation then is able to realise economies of scale.

Economies are most readily found in raw material supply, in production and distribution. Multinational marketing has been less easily seen as providing economies of scale, partly because of vested interest and complexity, and also because local needs are indeed often varied. Thus a company can find itself in the global arena without considering that its marketing could or should be coordinated beyond the loosest forms of management review. This certainly applied to the first generation of multinational companies growing up during the 1930s and the post-war years.

For such companies, the case for multinational marketing has by no means been self-evident, although most have gradually succumbed to some degree, under contemporary pressures. For the newer multinational operators, the trend towards international marketing, as well as the other functions like distribution, has been inevitable, not only for scale reasons. Among the forces at play are the legislative and political environments, and the need for speed of response to global competitive movements. Technical leadership in product manufacture is rarely sustainable beyond a short time-span, and manufacturing in any case has been confronted by retail power. Financial and city interests, educated in the worth of brands, also push companies towards developing coherent world-wide brand portfolios. Cost cutting and pressure on manpower combine to make the centralising trends irresistible.

The table below represents these worldwide business trends:

	Past	**Present/Future**
Economy	Predictable growth, local	Slow or no growth, world-wide
Market environment	Mass markets with known competitors and relatively fixed 'rules'	Stagnation in mass markets, aggressive competition
Products	Long production runs; production predictable	Segmentation and customisation mean more complex production
Technology	Few big companies, with R & D advantages	Technology available to all, lead times shortened
Political/legislative	Countries autonomous, no sharing of policies, little product legislation	Politics and legislation rapidly shared across borders and trading groups
Retail	Weak, dependent on manufacturer	Concentrated, powerful, own brands
Financial/city	Uninterested in company affairs beyond balance sheet; local	Knowledgeable and demanding, global in interests

THE PRESSURE TOWARDS COORDINATING COMMUNICATION PROGRAMMES

International advertising is not at all a foregone conclusion of multinational marketing. Many great multinational companies have hardly used it at all, even if they have strong underlying corporate philosophies and consistent business strategies (for example, Nestlé; some divisions of Unilever; Shell). Yet again, even for these well-entrenched companies, the pressures are there for communications to converge.

Within companies, good experienced people are in short supply. Most companies now are trying to take important marketing and advertising decisions at a more senior level, which means the number of decisions needs to be reduced. Centralised communications, including packaging, and direct marketing as well as advertising, if feasible, seem an attractive option at the top, and fit with the greater interest of the chairman's office in brands and their progress. Costly talent needs to be spread geographically to influence more markets. Expensive production costs can be pooled.

The same trends are found in advertising agencies and other marketing consultancies. Good ideas are scarce. Teams learn to operate in a looser-knit way, with production in one place, creative in another, and strategic leadership based in another. A small number of people, both in companies and agencies, increasingly bear responsibility for the brand's outward face, and call in specialist services as needed to support them, from research to packaging design.

Well-known market-place successes also demonstrate that coordination and harmonisation of advertising can work. Sometimes these cases demonstrate that advertising can even *lead* a multinational move. In 1970, Martini developed a highly innovate campaign with McCann-Erickson that was designed originally for the UK market.

But both the small family group owning the brand, and the agency, recognised that the campaign could work elsewhere. Thus, out of serendipity, developed a communications strategy which lifted the brand worldwide out of the aperitif sector into a class of its own. All countries were gradually brought under the coordination banner, with advertising production centrally controlled. Moreover, a blueprint existed to transfer to other markets, such as whisky, as Martini's corporate interests developed.

Media pressures are perhaps the strongest force of all for developing coordinated communication programmes, especially in Europe. In the past, mass market consumption and simple media structures prevailed, especially in the long period of television dominance, but the recent explosion of all media, and the growth of segmented, even fragmented or individual media usage has led to the search for consistent patterns, even if these are across borders.

INCREASING SIMILARITIES AMONG CONSUMERS

None of the trends outlined above would have relevance if consumers were not also becoming more alike from country to country.

Demographic trends are moving in similar directions everywhere in the developed world, even if the baselines are different across countries: stable or declining birth rates, ageing populations, declining youth cohorts. Trends associated with demography are also alike everywhere – for instance, rising divorce rates, smaller households, longer education, plus the affluence levels which support these trends – even the widening gap between affluent and poor.

Evidence has existed for many years now that social trends also cross borders – many originating outside Europe, in the US or (perhaps in the future) in Japan. Many of these trends are long-term and highly complex in effect, and we can only list some of them in a simplistic way here: interest in health and fitness, and the associated areas of nutritional knowledge, and alternative medicine; awareness of green issues; leisure pursuits as alternative outlets for creative, expressive or competitive instincts; the focus on women's roles and viewpoints; interest in local or community action; the home as a 'leisure centre'. These trends may show different manifestations by country and operate at different rates or levels, and thus necessitate different executional treatments at different points in time; but still the trends are present.

Sociologists generally agree that developed society has experienced a major change in values since the post-war years – indeed it would be surprising if this were not so. 'Post-industrial' society has moved towards an individual, experimental value system, away from inherited stable values concerning moral absolutes, with fixed views of the family and sex or class roles. 'Knowing your place' now has no place.

A diagram of social changes and the implications for marketing and communications might look like this:

	Past	Present/Future
Society's values	Stable values, moral absolutes, continuity, conformity	Individual, experimental values, importance of style, demonstration and change
People	Mass tastes, conformity, predictable lifestyles	Individual taste, expressivity, eclecticism
Communi-cation	1. Information, product benefits, rational mode (1950–70) 2. Lifestyle (1970–?)	Emotional expression, symbolism, metaphor

Some commentators have referred to the emergence of a 'new wave', or 'post modern consumer'. The writer's book on the McCann-Erickson European Youth Study, 1987, was among the first to comment on the phenomenon. That study contrasted the baby boomers' way of choosing brands with that of the new wave young, asserting that the new wave way was influencing others gradually and irresistibly.

The 'old' lifestyle way was for each 'type' of consumer to prefer products, goods and brands which fitted closely with its own characteristics or lifestyle. People from this generation struggled hard to identify who they were, and to define this in ways which would be recognisable both to themselves and to others. In the lifestyle era, different segments of baby boomers could be recognised by their views, their dress, their houses, their reading and viewing, and by the brands they chose. For older, more conservative and less advanced groups in society, such psychographic or lifestyle segmentation will persist.

But in post modern consumer attitudes, mix and match and eclecticism is the order of the day. Goods are used in an ephemeral way to express immediacy or empathy, from clothes to durables. The use of brands is the same. Brands which are well-known, liked and familiar may be used interchangeably, depending on prevailing feelings and what self-expression is wanted. New wave people do not *identify themselves* with the positioning in the same way that the lifestyle generation did; they recognise the positioning, but pick it up or put it down at will. It is thus of critical importance to be in the central 'evoked set' of brands. And it may be more important for modern brands to say something clear and meaningful, than to be executionally consistent over a period of time. Above all, the message needs saying now, in the language of the moment.

Post modern consumer attitudes are now apparent in all developed world markets, but they coexist with the older 'lifestyle' consumer attitudes and perhaps with the older-still 'mass market' consumer mentality (responding to product performance messages). It is clear that no single type of consumer typology or segmentation will describe all markets or all problems or all brands. It is more important for the communications expert, trying to make sense of a brand's consumer across borders, to be aware of the alternative interpretative frameworks which exist and to use each as relevant to the particular brand or problem.

Consumer classification systems in the future, therefore, will need to incorporate the appropriate mix for each brand of conventional demographics; psychographics, both general and tailored to the product field; geodemographics and other (eg observational) ways of codifying the way we live; plus an understanding of the more advanced consumption ethic, the 'buy-style' of the new wave consumer.

It is obviously important for marketing people to keep track of consumer trends. But the other half of the marketing equation, the brand and how it is perceived, is in many ways more important in the international context; especially with big brands with large consumer franchises. The consumer trends are the backdrop, the brands the protagonists.

We turn, therefore, to an examination of the brand and product field context and look at some common assumptions.

'My Product Field is Different from Yours'

The theory that different types of goods operate in different ways, using different consumer parameters and evoking different responses, has been a very persistent one.

At its simplest, people have argued that brands can be broadly grouped into 'functional' or 'representational' categories. 'Functional' brands demonstrate explicit product benefits, often performance-orientated, often rationally based, often in domestic or commodity spheres. 'Representational' brands, on the other hand, have little to differentiate them in physical benefit terms, often offer emotional rewards, often operate in the discretionary or even luxury sphere, and are individual rather than domestic purchases.

Many cases abound where this theory simply does not apply. Persil detergent is not a rationally-based brand, nor is Lux toilet soap; nor is PG Tips tea, nor Nescafé. The theory has fulfilled a useful role in providing a *post hoc* rationalisation for the logical/quantitative mode of working adopted by companies like P&G, and to 'justify' the difference in corporate culture which clearly exists between many companies in (say) the household products arena versus the fashion or alcoholic drinks fields.

But the theory has little to do with consumer perceptions. Packaged goods are as emotionally charged, as laden with symbolism and psychological meaning, as any other, as qualitative research can immediately demonstrate.

Differences in corporate culture actually underpin many theories apparently about market differences. For example, a feeling persists in marketing circles that food (in particular) is difficult to advertise using the same approach across borders. Yet there are cases of success which disprove the theory – from MacDonalds, via Del Monte canned fruit, to Sara Lee, to Möwenpick, to Buitoni. Foods of all types could probably use multinational advertising, if only the corporate will were there.

The reason why theories persist about food and other packaged goods being more 'difficult' than others to promote in a coordinated way is largely because until recently the owners of such packaged goods have not needed to coordinate their marketing. The vast majority of these brands, embedded in the fabric of people's daily lives, were marketed nationally in the past, when either people's lives truly *were* different from country to country, or the need to find the similarities did not exist. And reorganising the structural framework in which these companies operate – let alone the practical problems – is indeed difficult. But the consumer is not the problem.

Conversely, many multinational brands have already succeeded in newer product fields targeting the young, or the affluent – goods from jeans to rock music to CD players, to sports goods or computers have operated globally for some time. The reason is that, in general, the companies owning these brands *started* by operating globally, often using a small team and an entrepreneurial approach before this became a desirable and universal model of corporate excellence.

The Power of Corporate Culture

In our view, the single biggest factor determining how difficult a company finds international marketing and advertising is its corporate culture: what is its structural framework? Who holds the purse strings? Who makes the communications decisions – local or central departments? How many people or factions are involved? How long are the chains of command? In a nutshell, who has power?

It is possible to range multinational companies along a continuum, from largely local in operation, to fully international, as follows:

Decentralised, local, central management not concerned with controlling marketing strategy	Operate to central marketing guidelines but local freedom on detailed strategy and execution	Central strategy, local execution with input from centre	Central strategy and central execution

Companies can move themselves along the spectrum, with some effort and difficulty, as Black and Decker did during the late 1980s, from fully local to a form of central control. Other companies can stay local for a major portion of their activities, and centralise only when particular tasks or conditions apply – like Shell. Others have great local freedom in applying ideas from elsewhere, but still choose, for economy reasons or preference, to adopt the company line; this is the way in which Esso companies choose locally to use the tiger, or not (and most markets do, although the advertising briefs may be entirely different).

Other companies operate at different points on the continuum at the same time, depending on the product field and its history within the company. Thus, the Unilever margarine business operates with local freedom against broad central guidelines, but the detergents and toiletries divisions are more highly coordinated. Many large companies are allowing their traditional businesses only gradually to develop multinational advertising possibilities, but are operating new products or new divisions in a more centrally-controlled way.

Even in a highly coordinated company like Coca-Cola, where the corporate will towards centralising wherever possible is extremely strong at all levels and locations of the company, some local advertising decisions are made for smaller brands such as Tab or Five Alive.

A segmentation of companies suggests itself through the historical perspective:

1. Established multinationals – 'multi-local' operators. Often European in origins, they have set up local operations everywhere in the past and have developed local brands, albeit to a common culture and background strategy. Now looking for cost-cutting and efficiency, they are trying to rationalise brand portfolios and attempting common programmes for newer operations.

2. Established multinationals – branded goods in focused selected markets. Often US in origin, often in tobacco, alcoholic drinks or other beverages. Already have highly coordinated marketing and advertising, and worldwide brands. Usually have smaller brands run locally as well. Looking to develop or rationalise these; acquisition and NPD-conscious.

3. New multinationals – often European. Showing exporting mentalities, with limited local operations outside their home market, they are trying deliberately to find coordinated programmes which will also be acceptable locally, ie to change organically, taking as long as time and costs allow; may be overtaken by events and forced into painful changes.

4. New multinationals – often US-based. Lean operations, with travelling controllers, frequently reorganising their structures and relocating personnel. Can be in established goods or new technology fields, interested in acquisitions and NPD, only really interested in multinational branded products; they intend to be world players.

5. New multinationals – Japanese. Local operations very carefully set up to allow distribution, trading and marketing roots to be well-established, now beginning to look for further coordination possibilities in communications.

No doubt there are other sub-divisons to be constructed. The main virtue of the segmentation lies in its ability to focus the mind of the marketing person on the nature of the international or coordination need required; will the issues really be internal (ie company-originated), or external (ie consumer-originated)?

A RETHINK OF THE MARKETING AND ADVERTISING
PLANNING ROLE

Conventional thinking about brands operating across borders would suggest an immediate problem to the planner. By definition, the brand is going to be differently perceived by different types of consumer in each market. How, therefore, can it be the same brand everywhere? Even if its core values are the same, it may be at a different stage of development or in a different context, and this, conventionally, would change the indicated action.

Moreover, the marketing planner is trained to be the consumer representative within the brand team, whether this be inside the advertising agency or the company marketing department. If the consumer is a different consumer everywhere, which in some respects he or she is bound to be, then how can one properly plan the brand's future using the same response?

The answer is not to avoid the planning issue, but to find the planning perspective elsewhere. Big brands are *different*. A brand targeted tightly to its user works well only when it is new, or small, or occupying a niche, or perhaps a 'lifestyle' brand such as we have described. When a brand becomes an icon or international star, a name in its own right, a symbol and signifier of other meanings beyond its mere product form, then the responsibility becomes a different one. Then, the task is to present that pre-existing brand in the best possible light to the greatest number of people; to promote aspects which are appropriate. The responsibility is to display the brand, rather than to suit the consumer. In an international context, this difference in perspective is critical, or panic will follow.

Once the focus turns to the brand, it may prove to be, to all intents and purposes, the same everywhere. What varies is the competitive terrain in which it dwells. If our brand were (say) the Eiffel Tower, in its Paris context it would have a fine distinctiveness, albeit over-shadowed from some aspects by new buildings. If we put the Eiffel Tower in (say) Dublin, or Lisbon, it would astonish and be a singular landmark. But if it were deposited in mid-town Manhattan, it could well be virtually invisible. By analogy, the brand would have the same construction everywhere, but the competitive environment and the target market would vary. The core values would be constant, even if the advertising objectives were different.

Big international brands are often big and international simply because they have appeared to say the same thing in the same way to people over many years. They are not in the business of change, or of ephemeral effects; they seek maintenance and gradual renewal.

To renew such a brand with its consumers hardly noticing is a major task, especially when consumers feel they own the brand and its advertising, as they do with 'icon' brands. Consumers of these brands hate change and may well pan any new advertising, to the point where interpreting 'behind' the research becomes extremely difficult. There is a 'wear-in' effect. This is why middle-aged consumers still refer mistily to the Martini balloons commercial (from 1972), even though it would not bear close scrutiny today.

The question is, what is the advertising for an international brand supposed to do? Or, alternatively phrased, when is multinational advertising appropriate, and in what form?

Let us be clear that good multinational advertising does not mean going for the lowest common denominator. There may be local cultural and fashion traps to avoid, but this scarcely closes the creative door at all, since there are so many other rich seams to mine – often tapping into the real, absolute, expressive or basic emotions which are common to all of us. With big brands it is perverse to sneer at the obvious.

UNDERSTANDING THE BRAND ACROSS BORDERS

The most enduring brand personalities – whether they use a property like the Esso tiger, or an archetype such as the Viennetta party, or a myth such as the Levi's advertising – express what the brand is through a distinctive blend of the functional and emotional components.

Understanding the brand at the multinational level may be more cumbersome and more expensive than understanding it at the local level, but the mechanics are largely similar. As usual, the process breaks down into two phases, the conceptual planning phase and the operational.

The conceptual planning phase covers several stages, from determining which brands are (most) appropriate for which markets, through to discovering which brand messages would best be communicated to which audiences. Typically, this is a consumer research driven phase, examining both the in-house and competitive brands. And centrally-planned research to a common format and executed with well-briefed and controlled fieldwork, whether qualitative or quantitative, is more likely to produce answers without irrelevant 'noise' than research bought and briefed *ad hoc* on a market-by-market basis.

Once the brand message has been clarified, the particular company structure or culture will determine how the operational stage will be executed, from central to local on the continuum, as we have already discussed. Let us repeat that the reason for concentrating on the brand rather than the consumer, as the primary task, is to understand the unique personality, the thumb-print of our particular brand, in order to display it at its most effective to the greatest number of people.

Planning Brand Advertising across Borders

At the conceptual level there are, as we have indicated already, many frameworks known to the research and planning fraternity which can help us to understand the nature of the brand, and to establish its core values. One framework which has been particularly useful in the multinational context is that of the three constants: does the brand have a constant product function, personality, and advertising identity? To describe the structure further:

Product function or performance: At the most basic or prosaic level, the question of how the brand 'works' needs describing. The brand's status as a physical product is the traditional area of the USP, and the field where in the past many marketing people sought to create abiding differences between brands. In many product fields, folk memories of past physical or performance claims live on ('She can't tell Stork from butter', 'Guinness is good for you'). In virtually all product fields, product performance remains an important *perceived* area of brand delivery. Consumers use product language easily, often as an analogy to describe their feelings. Brands people love and are loyal to will tend to have the highest product ratings. Yet in some fields, product functional ratings barely discriminate between brands, nor do they shift over time as brand shares change.

But in other areas, product values may still swing brand choice. In fields as diverse as power tools or chocolate count lines, the physical performance or experience of the brand, whether real or perceived, is key to understanding that brand. If a power tool brand gets rated as tinny, noisy and lightweight, we know it is a loser before we know anything about its personality.

In the international context, we should discover whether the product is the same everywhere, or does it differ in specification according to local requirements? Is this important? What does the product do to or for people. What are the functional benefits or rewards it offers? Are these the same everywhere?

Brand personality: We have already pointed out that the *brand's* personality is a different concept from the *user's* personality, and that our focus will be primarily on the brand.

Sometimes the user's and the brand's personality will coincide, as with 'lifestyle' brands and (for example) some car brand purchases. But in many categories, the user and brand personalities will not coincide. The concept of mix and match – fitting brands to needstyle – is often more appropriate: people buy different brands in different modes, and sometimes they simply rotate through their central 'set'.

Some whole categories may be bought for display or 'badging' purposes, particularly youth brands. Other brands may be chosen because their 'personalities' stand as a metaphor for the product function: as with the Lux toilet soap personality representing the ideal bath – luxurious, renewing, beautifying, pampering. Other brand personalities represent moral virtues, like Volvo or Body Shop. Others are authority figures standing for reassurance and familiarity, such as Persil.

Brand personality is often also called brand character. Traditionally, the field of brand personality has been explored qualitatively, using projective techniques such as trigger boards, 'psychodoodles' etc, but brand character can also relatively easily be quantified.

Other facets of brand character, in addition to that of brand personality alone, can be extremely revealing. One area is that of perceived user stereotypes (NB not the same as *actual* user). If we say 'career girl' or 'truck driver' to you, it is probable that, despite your no doubt entirely legitimate protestations about the artificiality of stereotypes, you would have quite a similar picture in your mind to the picture in the mind of the person sitting next to you. Such labels work as a shorthand, a currency in our media-saturated cultures, and therefore function well as brand discriminators.

Similarly, a brand's temperament or mood can be explored: its perceived pace, temperature, or distance. Such tonal qualifiers, importantly, begin to take us into the world of evaluation of what the personality of the brand *means*. Is the brand, however it is described, experienced as warm, measured in pace, close to me and moving closer – or is it slow, cold, unreachable? If we described a brand as sophisticted and showy, and liked by model girls, you would not know for sure how we felt about it unless we also found a way of telling you that we felt comfortable and light-hearted with the brand, rather than intimidated and distant.

Further aspects of brand character develop from an anthropological approach, in understanding human archetypes and symbolism. This is especially relevant to brand benefits in the fields of self-expression, creativity, narcissism, posing and display. Anthropologists have described male and female archetypes (the Prince, the Macho Male, the Princess, the Female Hero, etc), and they have also described universal myths or symbols (such as the search for eternal life, superman, etc) which can help us understand better the basis of brands' appeals to different needstyles of consumer.

In the international context, the key questions are, what personality characteristics are displayed by the brand and its advertising? If it were a person, how would it be described? Do the same people use the same vocabulary and metaphors across borders? What is the key emotional link between the brand and its user? On what level does this exist – at the archetypal, or the moral, or the playful, or the practical? In what mode do people use the brand? Is this the same everywhere?

The advertising identity of the brand: All established brands, whether global or local, have a set of advertising conventions. A look at the reel of commercials from the past, or across countries, will tend to reveal a common advertising style, which survives despite different strategies emphasising different features of the brand message at different times or places.

Sometimes, this issue of style is codified by the company, sometimes not. Most international brands have sets of 'rules' or conventions written down, but some – especially new ones or those in evolution – may operate more informally.

Some advertising ideas cross borders easily, while others do not. These can be represented diagrammatically:

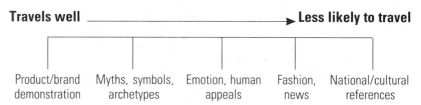

Travels well ⎯⎯⎯⎯⎯⎯⎯⎯⎯⎯⎯⎯⎯⎯⎯⎯⟶ **Less likely to travel**

| Product/brand demonstration | Myths, symbols, archetypes | Emotion, human appeals | Fashion, news | National/cultural references |

We have described above three aspects of the brand which should be perceived as, and kept, constant, if the core brand is truly to be international: its product function; its character and how consumers relate to it; and its advertising style. These are the three constants to international core brand values:

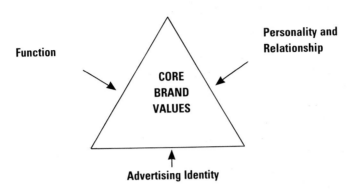

There are two other aspects of the international brand, which may actually need to *vary* over time and/or place (as Stephen Hawking has proposed, time and space are interchangeable – as international brands demonstrate). These aspects will help determine whether the same advertisement can be run at the same time everywhere, or whether the brand has to be seen as moving along a continuum, at a different point in its life cycle in different places: as it were in a different landscape, as with our transporting of the Eiffel Tower. In some cases, a pool of commercials may be planned for, or tactical deviations from the mainstream brand advertising made for particular purposes, even if the core values remain constant.

These two aspects are, first, a consideration of the role of the advertising, and second (and not always necessary) an account of any relevant cultural differences or requirements.

The question of the advertising's specific role is quite likely to vary from market to market, as a result of the brand's life cycle and differing competitive needs. Is the target audience the same everywhere (new users, lapsed users, young people)? Is the advertising trying to grow the brand, increase awareness, build share – or is it a brand maintenance situation? Does this vary across countries? With most international brands, it is possible to group markets into those in development mode and those in maintenance, or even decline, and determine whether one, or two or even three 'versions' of the brand's advertising will be required to cover the spectrum of needs.

The second variable aspect, that of reflecting cultural requirements, tends to be easily evident from research, if it is of real importance. Coca-Cola has been known to stratify its 'pool' of commercials by climatic factors, beach scenarios being important in hot climates but less so in Europe. Legal requirements may vary, and undoubtedly cultural stereotypes do exist (although these are often dangerous and misleading). However, big international brands usually operate at the non-cultural, non-fashion end of the spectrum of advertising styles already described, and frequently cultural factors turn out in practice to be of minor relevance.

The exception is the often-codified difference between the home market and all others. Many international brands preserve, for historical, cultural, organisational and even consumer reasons, a distinction between 'domestic' and 'international' markets. Having learned early on that straightforward advertising and communications exports may not work, marketing people have maintained the difference between the brand at home and the brand abroad. Home markets may indeed be more strongly established, more entrenched, larger, more specifically rooted in the culture, or more sophisticated; and consumers may indeed feel differently about a brand known to be 'invented here' – as Perrier demonstrates in France, or Coca-Cola in the US, or Guinness in Ireland, or many whisky brands in the UK.

Multinational brand marketing above all takes experience, objectivity and optimism. Experience tells when cultural issues arise: are they important or not? Is the long-term gain more important than the short-term advantage? Objectivity is vital when politics intervene. Brand owners often *do* know their brands best; they often have a grasp of the long-term issues, and the consumer's immediate views may or may not always feature in this – to an agency's chagrin. And optimism is not only a need, but a by-product. There is no more rewarding role in marketing than having a piece of the action in planning the future of the big brands in the top world league.

Index